THE COMPLETE BARBECUE BOOK

The Complete
Barbecue Book

I'M THE CHEF!

By *JOHN* and MARIE ROBERSON

Illustrated by H. W. DOREMUS

PRENTICE-HALL, INC.

NEW YORK

CONTENTS

ix

x

FOREWORD

Inventive cooking is definitely a *man's* approach to the preparation of food. It is the method that any man with a flair for food and cooking—who is not addicted to the use of ordinary household cookbooks—uses when he proceeds to barbecue. At this moment in his culinary experiences, he steps smack into the realm of true adventure.

Now, thanks to John and Marie Roberson whose loving and inspired efforts have made possible this remarkable guide to outdoor cooking, *The Complete Barbecue Book*—a man can really use his imagination—*create*—as he cooks. For here he has a safe and sure guide to his every step. He has everything he needs to know, including a wide range of outstanding barbecue recipes. Even if he is utterly without experience, from these pages he can sally forth as an expert in the art of barbecuing.

Because of my many contacts with members of The Society Of Amateur Chefs, from New York to Hollywood and back again, I believe I can safely say that *here* is the complete barbecue cookbook for which all have been waiting. So much of the Amateur Chefs' cooking is done al fresco. Their many problems, heretofore only vaguely answered, now are solved in what will, in my opinion, prove a veritable cooking "bible" for our clan. I lift my best spatula in an enthusiastic salute to this farsighted Greenwich, Connecticut couple who here have contributed so ably and so well toward better outdoor cooking and dining!

I know that Jack Dempsey, Lauritz Melchior, Russell Patterson, Bradshaw Crandell, Rube Goldberg, Hinson Stiles, Dean Cornwell and other worthies of our society will join

me in paying this well-earned tribute to Mr. and Mr.
Roberson.

For less than the cost of a sirloin steak for a party of six,
the Robersons have given us in *The Complete Barbecue
Book* an insurance policy guaranteeing everlasting fun and
success before the open pit or grill.

Bon appetit à vous, Monsieur et Madame Roberson!

Gustatorially yours,

BEN IRVIN BUTLER
Founder and President
The Society of Amateur Chefs

ACKNOWLEDGMENTS

We wish to acknowledge with many thanks the splendid cooperation from the following firms and groups for their ideas and suggestions:

James T. Brown of Hawaii
Mrs. George C. Kellogg of California
Mrs. Eben Learned of Connecticut
Ohio Stove Company
Glen Hall Brands
Poultry and Egg National Board
Angostura Wupperman Corp.
American Meat Institute
Society of Amateur Chefs
McIlhenny Tabasco Sauce Co.
Majestic Company
Adolf Eccardt
Eclipse Metal Manufacturing Company
United States Brewers Foundation
Charles Schaefer and Son, Inc.
Hillbro Crafts
Dole Hawaiian Pineapple Products
G. F. Heublein and Bro., Inc.
Charles Gulden, Inc.
American Spice Trade Assn.

And many other friends whose kind suggestions helped to make this book possible.

THE COMPLETE BARBECUE BOOK

Things You'll Need to Know

Fire—the Heavenly Gift

If man still worshiped a galaxy of ancient gods as he did of old, high on his list of deities would loom the Titan, Prometheus. Legend tells us it was he who stole fire from heaven and gave it to lowly, much-neglected man. But even great Zeus, though then enraged and frustrated, must have mellowed considerably through all the years as he observed at least *one* use man has made of fire, the heavenly gift. We refer, of course, to man's cooking with fire outdoors—the barbecue.

Old Zeus would doff his halo with jaunty aplomb to the modern man, expert or neophyte, who explores with us the joyous art of barbecuing and here learns how it is done. It's so easy and so much fun! Once the scent of meat a-cookin' amid wood smoke gets into your nostrils, you'll become a

1

changed man. You will take on a somewhat godlike stature. Your every performance before pit or grill will both please the eyes and tickle the palates of the lucky guests who sample your culinary handiwork. As for the ladies—well, they'll virtually be your slaves, for, bless 'em, they know that barbecuing is a *man's* hobby. They are lavish in the homage they pay to him who knows *how*. In fact, once women see you turn out any of these foods for the gods which our time-tried recipes make possible, you will always have their help with the less glamorous chores, like paring vegetables, setting tables, etc.

Barbecue History

The very history of barbecuing establishes it as primarily a man's occupation. Some authorities claim that the word "barbecue" was coined by seventeenth-century French corsairs, who termed it *"de barbe à cue,"* which literally means cooked from "beard to tail." Certain dictionary writers were apparently misled when they claimed it was derived from the Spanish word *barbacoa,* an offshoot from a native Haitian word for a wood framework used as a grill, a not-too-inadequate bedstead, or a rack for drying foods. For one thing, there isn't any such word in Castilian or any other Spanish dialect. It is pure Mexican, and we're convinced it came straight from the native Indians of the Mississippi valley. This contribution to barbecue history is gleaned from a book written by an eighteenth-century French officer, Jean Bernard Bossu, an adventurer who visited the Mississippi area some two hundred years ago. Bossu actually attended one of these *fêtes champêtres* with a large gathering of white and colored people, and wrote, *"le plat de fondation est un cochon maron que l'on fait griller tout entier sur les charbons."*

Dictionary writers may have based their definition upon information contained in a book, *Anahuac, or Mexico and the Mexicans,* by Sir Edward Burnett Tyler, a renowned anthropologist of his era. In notes on a trip to Mexico in 1856, Tyler mentions witnessing a native barbecue and assumes the word had evolved through Spanish from the Haitian *babracot,* meaning any sort of wooden framework. To quote a passage from Sir Edward's book, he says that one of the Mexicans "invited a party of neighbors to eat up a kid that had been covered in a hole in the ground with embers upon it after the Sandwich Island fashion. This is called a *barbacoa.*"

Whether they belong to the "who-cares" school of thought as to the word's origin, the first thing that pops into the heads of most Americans nowadays if you say "barbecue" is the vision of a peppery sauce with vinegar and tomato, and the iniquitous but ever-present "Bar-B-Q" emporium. There is usually a secondary impression of roasted meat. A century ago, however, when barbecuing became a really important phase of American cookery, the emphasis was not on the sauce. To most of our forefathers, north, south, east or west, barbecue suggested a large outdoor gathering. Political speeches and a band were as essential as the feast of roasted meats itself.

Harper's Weekly for October, 1896, describes the barbecues in vogue at that time. It tells us that, "asked to define the whole duty of a man in a political year, nine out of ten persons in the South or Middle West would say, 'to holler right, vote straight, and eat as much barbecue as any other man in the county.' " No doubt this form of entertainment smoothed and softened campaign asperities.

The barbecues of that day seem generally to have been non-partisan affairs. That is, members of both political parties came to the same gatherings, with the leaders of each faction competing with one another to supply the largest contributions of food and drink. Folk gathered from far and near, rising at dawn to reach the appointed place in time for the speeches and band concert. Preparations for the feast began much earlier—sometimes days in advance. There were no hors d'oeuvres or advance refreshments, no appetizers or cocktails such as we moderns sometimes find at hand. Then everyone arrived half-starved, eager for the succulent main courses. When you ordered your beef by the drove and lamb by the flock, you gave short shrift to such non-essentials.

During the speech-making, aides of the speakers circulated among the audience, leading the CHEERS, APPLAUSE, and LOUD LAUGHTER. Sometimes they stood about, half-hidden in the background, to observe guests' reactions and report to the dais when listeners became indifferent.

According to *Harper's Weekly*, the meat was roasted whole or in quarters. Branches of sassafras wood were cut and whittled to sharp points. These were used as spits, their ends extending over the edges of the pits in which the fires were built. While the roasting was going on, the meat was basted only with hot salted water. At the end, when the meat was on the carving table, it was daubed with "dipney"—sweet country lard and the strongest vinegar, seasoned with red and black pepper. It was so peppery hot that it brought tears to the eyes of novices. Also, these outdoor banquets were "not to be insulted by the company of cakes and kickshaws of the usual picnic variety!" The only accompaniment to the roast meat was thick slices of the best bread that could be had— also cucumbers, fresh and pickled.

Diners then, as now, ate until they had satisfied their appetites in good Homeric fashion. After the food came piping hot black coffee with two neat fingers of brandy or the finest old whiskey. It was customary also to provide plenty of beer or wine throughout the meal.

An article by D. A. Willey in a bygone English magazine, *Wide World*, refers to "curious functions in the United States called barbecues, during which entire herds of cattle and flocks of sheep are slaughtered to feed the guests, and as many as six thousand people sit down at once." With typical British understatement, Willey describes this as a "rather large dinner party." He also mentions a "great commercial travelers' barbecue at Atlanta, Ga., at which one thousand persons sat down at the same time."

This British one-time sojourner in America mentions barbecue stew as an important adjunct to the roasted meat. According to him, this was prepared in the North in kettles

4

used for boiling maple sugar. In the South, other enormous kettles, often holding as much as fifty gallons, were forged especially for barbecues. When the animals were cut up, scrap meat and the bones were put into these kettles, together with certain vegetables, herbs, and other seasonings. Then the kettles were hung from tripods. There was an air of secrecy about concoctions used in flavoring meats. Old plantation negroes were specialists in preparing these and in directing the roasting of the meat. They were persons of importance at barbecues, often appearing in frock coats and supervising other old negroes "whose hair had turned white bending over smoking trenches where meat is cooked."

In the South, the barbecue frequently was a one-party political affair, candidates vying with each other to provide the best offering of foods.

Sheep were cut in half, beef in quarters, and pigs roasted whole, much as in our large barbecues of today. Sweet potatoes and corn were frequently served with the meat. Plates were laid out on long tables, and as soon as the meat was roasted it was carved with amazing speed, placed upon plates with thick slices of bread, and served so that the guests could eat as quickly as possible. Everyone began at once. The stew was put into bowls and arranged on tables for diners to help themselves. Plates were refilled as soon as emptied, without so much as a by-your-leave. (A good custom to follow nowadays!)

Willey describes preparations, including the digging of trenches from two to seven feet wide and from one to three feet in depth: "Straight branches are peeled of bark and knots, and sharpened at the ends. The animals are pierced lengthwise and arranged so that ends of sticks extend over the side of the trench. In the meantime, fires have been laid in the trenches. Pieces of pine wood are mixed with shavings at the bottom, then hardwood. After the meat has been placed upon the cross sticks, a signal is given and all trenches are lighted at once. Great expertness is needed to keep the fires burning evenly. When partly done on one side, the meat is flopped—not turned—as on a metal spit. Flopping must be done only by experienced hands. Special knives and cleavers are used for cutting up the meat."

Perhaps someday our historians, instead of lauding political bigwigs of the past for their oratorical eloquence, will tell us more about the influence of their barbecues upon the hearts and minds of the American populace. At any rate, today we can cook with the gusto of native past masters, use their recipes, now much improved, and enjoy barbecuing of a character and excellence they could never have known.

So, with this much barbecue lore for background, let us done chefs' caps and aprons and go now into the "meat" of this romantic modern—yet ancient—business of cooking outdoors, as it is done by twentieth-century knights of the pit and grill. Let us match skillets in this fascinating he-man fun and learn how to barbecue *au fait*—easily and expertly.

Barbecuing—an Adventure

Fire, fuel, and food are the three *sine qua non*s or withoutwhichs of barbecuing. In other words, if we had some fuel, if we had a light, if we had some food, we'd have a feast—that is, if we had what it takes in the way of equipment. The entire story of cookery since man or near-man (for *Homo* wasn't even *Sapiens* at that remote date) began has been a working-out of that problem. Interestingly enough, when humans first went to work with fire and food, they invented or discovered every style of cooking now known. So far as methods go, there is nothing left for the home cooks, chefs and "home-ec" gals to do—that is, in the way of basic principles—in roasting, baking, grilling, frying, steaming, pressure-cooking, etc. It was all figured out before civilization.

Cooking began practically without equipment—and as part of your own adventure in barbecuing, you might do the same. There is, in fact, the purist school of amateurs, which holds to the notion that the fewer and more primitive your tools, the more authentic your barbecue results. In our opinion, that kind of ultra-orthodoxy is tiresome. It has spoiled many a barbecue party. You know—the self-styled expert who insists upon doing everything the hard way rather than make use of modern equipment or gadgetry. It is our contention that the real masters are men who take advantage of any twentieth-century short-cut, even to an electrically turned roasting spit, so long as there is nothing to spoil the fun or the flavor.

By way of adventure, then, let us start from the beginning—with the three F's—fire, fuel and food. Like early man you look about in search of make-do, and all you see are trees and leaves, sticks, stones, sand, mud or clay, and, we hope, a bubbling brook of clear water. There you are. You take a stick, peel off its bark, thrust it through your fish or bird, and presto! you have a spit upon which to hold your food to the flame without burning your fingers. If your morsel drops in the fire, the flames, with as good an appetite as your own, devour it pronto. But if by accident it drops on the hot—but not *burning*—embers, you have the first step in roasting. Stones and rocks, you discover, hold the heat without burning the food. And if you wrap your tidbit in leaves or mold it in a few handfuls of wet clay, you can achieve even better results.

The Matter of Spits

But to get back to the hand-held wooden spit. It was quick and fairly safe, but it was time-consuming. While you held the spit, you couldn't do anything else. If you could rig up some device to hold the spit, you would free your hands to tend the fire and do other things. So you hit upon the idea of building up props of stones, one on each side of the fire, and placing your stick with the ends supported by these stone props. Better still, you'd dig a hole in the earth, build your fire in the hole, and use the sides of the pit to support the ends of your stick. By building your pit longer, you could arrange several spits over the same fire.

For lack of anything better, or just for the heck of it, you can still use a wooden stick. Use a freshly cut, straight twig, which resists heat and fire better than wood that has been cut and partially dried. Branches of sassafras trees, barked and pointed, are the best. Obviously, however, metal spits are to be preferred and are basic items in *your* barbecue kit.

In the early days of barbecue cookery, long spits were arranged over pit fires. This over-the-fire cooking had the disadvantage of wasting the precious, flavor-filled, and healthful juices. For this reason, many barbecue experts now prefer beside-the-fire spitting, because in this way juices do not fall on the fire. Instead, they may be caught in a tray placed beneath the roasting meat. When you shop for barbecue equipment, you'll find a number of devices for conserving these essential juices.

In early American pit-and-spit roasting, the pieces of meat had to be turned at frequent intervals or flopped to insure even cooking. Long before that, however, cooks had struck upon the idea of using a wheel turned by a dog or small boy. In old England these spits were manipulated by the aged and beggars, eager to obtain scraps of food to keep body and soul together. It was in Tudor England that the human motive power was supplanted by canine energy. Geese were likewise employed in France during the reign of Louis XIV. Later, during Charles II's reign as king of England, clockwork came into being. These devices were so ingenious that they not only operated the turning spits, but even timed the roasting period to suit lordly tastes. A certain Lord Keeper by the name of Guilford is said to have owned a clockwork arrangement that cost him thirty pounds, and he toted it along on all his many travels, setting it up in inns and castles wherever he went. Along about this time there was, believe it or not, a musical turning spit, the timing of which only a chef with a musical ear could handle. So many notes and bars and the roast was done—so many the fowl—so many more and the dinner itself!

The end of the eighteenth century saw the last of human or canine turnspits and the beginning of the smoke jack— an arrangement of fans and drafts. A gravity system, wherein the weight of the meat rotated the spit, also became popular. Our present-day equipment shows wheel devices you can turn by hand and electrically rotated spits for use indoors or out. Certainly no one can say that this dash of modernity detracts from the genuine barbecue flavor.

The Grate or Grill

An obvious outcome of the spit was the grate or grill—a series of small spits placed in combination over the fire instead of one. This made possible the roasting or broiling of smaller morsels that could not so well be impaled on a single spit. It also provided a solid frame upon which to set pans for frying, boiling, or warming of food.

Here is a good suggestion: if you lack a specially made grill, you can use as a makeshift a bit of heavy screening stretched over your pit fire. You can also borrow an iron grating from your gas or electric range for this purpose.

And just as you have your smart shish-kebab-skewer sets as up-to-date versions of primitive spit-cooking, so you also have your portable charcoal-burning steak-and-chop broilers as the very latest echo of the old-time iron grill or wire broiler.

The sky's the limit—not to mention your bank account—when it comes to well-contrived barbecue equipment. Remember that many types of outdoor cooking can be done in the primitive way for practically no financial outlay, or in the plush way for as much as you possess. Old or new, primitive or modern—it makes no great difference. All that does matter is the *flavor* of your cuisine—plus an opportunity for a stimulating bit of showmanship and make-believe. Our advice is to visit one of the gourmet shops, department or hardware stores where such merchandise is sold, or stay at home and read the manufacturers' catalogues. The latter make mighty good reading for amateur outdoor chefs.

After—or probably before—you take stock of such portable equipment, you should consider the *where* and *how* of a more stationary, permanent barbecue.

One of the most agreeable features of present-day barbecue development, it seems to us, is that the set-up is usually fairly near your own back door. You enjoy the flavor and, we hope, the fervor of outdoor cooking and dining without the fuss and muss of a picnic. What blend of outdoors and indoors you want in your barbecue setting depends not only upon your personal taste and architectural background, but upon climate as well.

Here are the various types of "fire places"—using the term broadly, as a place in which to put your fire and upon which to perform your barbecuing rites.

Pit Barbecue

This is perhaps the easiest, cheapest, and most primitive kind of fire place. It may be round, square, or oblong. For an impromptu, temporary affair, you simply dig a hole of desired shape and size, taking care to locate the "diggings" far enough away from your excavation so that they won't interfere with your fire-tending or cooking later on. The size, of course, depends on the number you will feed. If you're planning to roast a whole side of beef for a platoon of ravenous friends, relatives and henchmen, you are advised to dig a trench 40 inches deep, three feet wide, and ten feet long.

Pit-cooking is really something of a specialty in itself, dating back to prehistoric days when men discovered they didn't need an open, active fire to cook food. So they dug their holes, lined them with hot embers, wrapped their fish in seaweed or their birds in grape leaves, then placed them in the hole, adding more hot embers and such covering as they could obtain—first wood, and later on, as civilization progressed, metal sheets. To prevent burning, a layer of dry sand was often inserted between the embers and the food.

From such a cooking procedure came at length the fireless cooker and more recently the pressure cooker. With a permanent, well-constructed fire pit in his patio or garden, the up-to-date barbecue chef now can perform all sorts of culinary tricks: baked beans, roasted meats and vegetables, and so on.

One of the best ways to roast beef is in a fire pit of this sort. It's truly down to earth, even if it does taste "out of this world." The meat is wrapped in two thicknesses of cheesecloth, securely tied and then wrapped in burlap. Clean, dry sand is placed over the embers and on top of the meat, then more embers, and finally the sheet-iron cover. It's kickin' good, though nothing for the short-order cook, since it takes a large piece of meat eight or ten hours to cook.

For something a little cozier and more permanent, you can make a much smaller excavation, lining it with fire bricks or stones. As we have just pointed out, these pits are generally round or square, and size and shape are planned to correspond with the grill and other equipment you plan to use along with them. As a practical suggestion, such a pit may be utilized as a trash burner after the feast is over. In this case, to be sure, it must always be thoroughly cleaned of all refuse before being put to use in barbecuing later on.

Brick or Stone Fireplace

Literally one or two steps up from the simple pit is the brick or stone fireplace, which provides back and side protection for your fire as well as a firm base upon which to set your spits and grills. The fire is tended from the front without interfering with what is cooking on top.

Build your bricks or stones a bit higher off the ground—about four inches—and you can accomplish your culinary magic without stooping, bending, or squatting. The additional height also makes it possible for you to have a fuel grate upon which to lay your fire, with space for ashes below. With more bricks and stones and a little added ingenuity on your part, you can erect a chimney at the back. Presto—you then have an actual stove which, with a few more bricks, will provide an oven and dish-warming space. (See illustration, page 33.) For such a stove-shaped cooker, the chimney is logically built in the rear, thus leaving the top for grill or other surface cooking space. If you choose, you can build the chimney straight up from the fire and in this way create an open fireplace at the front with just the right arrangement for beside-the-fire spit-cooking.

Of course there are all sorts of grills and grates, facings, linings and other what-nots available at your barbecue-specialty dealer's, or at sports and hardware stores.

If you have difficulty in deciding exactly which type of cooking place you want, your best bet may be to experiment. At any rate, the round or square pit offers a worth-while supplement to either the stove or open-fireplace style of construction.

Deciding About Equipment

Now with this general philosophy of the technique of cooking *al fresco* in mind, let us help you further in deciding upon the most practical type of barbecue arrangement to own. Of course it is up to you to select the kind best suited to your particular needs: a simple garden or patio grill (page 32), a fireplace barbecue, an open-air kitchen or an outdoor-indoor barbecue, the latter being a prefabricated, portable piece of apparatus. You can build any of the first three from the simplest to the more elaborate yourself, if you are handy with tools and follow the simple directions we give you on pages 32-35. Be sure, however, to locate your pit or grill in the direction of prevailing winds to prevent smoke from constantly blowing in the faces of your family or friends. (See "Do's and Don'ts," page 21.) If you do not construct your own barbecue, on the other hand, then you will need to consult a competent builder or contractor. In such case, show him one of our plan suggestions (pages 37, 38). Discuss with him your individual problems and needs. We may only add again that it is advisable to secure a number of barbecue catalogues from your nearby dealer or by writing to manufacturers who advertise in leading gardening and home magazines. Then, last but not least, you have a wide selection of portable equipment to pick from: horizontal, vertical, with spits that may be turned by hand, by clockwork, or by electricity. Many of these also are usable indoors during the long winter months, when cooking in patio or garden is impracticable. You will note that our Equipment Section includes an inexpensive small grill that fits into your fireplace, as well as a complete barbecue machine for every cooking purpose.

Essentials to Know

A simple, functional outdoor cookstove is basically a large square chimney of bricks approximately four feet high. It has a good-sized firebox with grill over it and will cook four or five steaks or six chickens split for broiling at the same time. Under the firebox is ample storage space. The more efficient outdoor range has a stainless-steel top with welded edge that fits over the grill. This contains a small vent and a flue for proper fire draw. Such a stove is excellent for assembly-line production, and on it you can cook everything from a raft of hamburgers to bacon, eggs, and hot cakes.

Besides the different kinds of grills or pits so far discussed, you will want to consider the various manufacturing outfits which are on the market today. We favor a particular type of vertical grill with spits which was first brought out several years ago. It is marvelous for roasting, grilling, or broiling. It follows the principles of fireplaces that still are in use after centuries in many of the old houses of Europe and America. Further, this type is as useful as an electric range. Most models of this type have a good-sized vertical firebox for coals, and grills that suspend in front for broiling or grilling. All have steel spits upon which you can roast anything from a quail to a small suckling pig with a minimum of effort and a maximum of mouth-watering results. Some operate by clockwork or hand; others are motor-driven.

Then there are the horizontal types with a spit which may be built into any style of fireplace, but which provide the same degree of accommodation as above. These have several advantages in their favor.

One complete outdoor fireplace has a large fuel box and supply closets flanking both sides. These may be kept as well-stocked as your kitchen shelves. Some such units include a work table—though we have a warm spot in our hearts for the portable, folding table shown on page 53. It is handy for every need, and not only on your own premises—it may be stowed away in your car for trips, fishing, swimming, camping, or wherever you are apt to do some outdoor cooking. Units that do include a work table also have a sink with spacious metal drain boards. At right angles, there may be room for a four-burner electric range with oven, and a full-sized refrigerator; drawers for equipment and closets for dishes. Take a glance at page 38 if you want to see an aristocrat in the way of barbecue equipment of this caliber. There's no bothersome traipsing back and forth to the kitchen for ice cubes, bottle or can openers, or another plate with this elaborate job. Hollywood, take note!!

If you invest in equipment of de luxe proportions, you will necessarily want to make certain that shut-offs for your utilities and well-insulated weatherproof covers are provided for all-year-around weather protection.

The Dutch Oven

Here is an item we especially want to bring to your attention. For barbecuing, there is only one sort of Dutch oven. That is a sturdy, cast-iron utensil, with a solid close-fitting cover and a strong semi-circular handle, from one side to the other, by which the oven may be lifted or hung on a crane over the fire. If you plan to do considerable cooking à la barbecue, you really should include this utilitarian device.

Credit, Griswold Mfg. Co.

Besides the all-metal Dutch ovens, a majority of the stores have those that are equipped with heavy glass covers. The advantage of these is that they enable you to see what's going on inside without removing the lid. As a matter of fact, some cast-iron Dutch ovens now have glass covers, but it is our observation that most barbecuing is done with the solid metal ovens, merely because of the possibility (remote though it may be) of the glass getting broken in outdoor use.

It would be very difficult to find a more versatile utensil than the Dutch oven. When first conceived it really was an oven, to be placed in hot embers with glowing coals packed on top in order to ensure slow, even "baking."

Sophisticates among outdoor chefs praise the Dutch oven for hole-in-the-ground cookery. The hole in this case should be somewhat larger than the oven and lined with stones or fire bricks. Build your fire, and when you have heated the stones, rake out the embers—all except a bottom layer two inches deep. Then drop your oven in the hole, cover attached, shovel hot embers around its sides, and again stack embers or hot stones on top. Cover with a metal sheet and let 'er go. Six or seven, or maybe as much as ten hours later—dependent, of course, upon what you are cooking—your dish will be done to an epicurean turn. We have found it often a good idea to turn the oven lid over (upside down) so that its concave side will be on top. This holds the hot stones or embers more readily than the convex side. And it's actually no more trouble to scour this side than the other later on.

Then, too, there is nothing finer than a Dutch oven for cooking over an open campfire, providing you have a tripod or a portable crane strong enough to carry the weight of a heavy metal oven or kettle. The solid metal and close-fitting cover make for slow, even cooking. For any kind of meat-cooking, whether you use your oven on an open-air fire or on your gas or electric range, the results will be always the same. First step is to drop a bit of fat—butter, bacon drippings, suet, vegetable oil, or shortening—in the Dutch oven. Melt and heat this without browning. Next, have your oven good and hot when you put in your meat, which has previously been dredged with flour and seasoned with salt and pepper. In browning, be sure to sear first one side and then all the other surfaces of your meat. When this is done and all sides are nicely browned, add a cup of water, replace the cover of your oven, and cook slowly. You will find that there is practically no evaporation if you keep your oven covered throughout the cooking process; therefore your meat will remain moist without the addition of more water.

Onions, carrots, celery, and other vegetables may be added after the meat is half cooked.

In cooking a pot roast in your Dutch oven, you can brown the meat beforehand as outlined above, except that you must allow more time for the browning process and then do the slow cooking in the oven afterwards; or you can simmer the meat first in a little water and brown it at the end. To accomplish this, you remove the meat and any vegetables you may have added and set them aside. Then you sprinkle flour over the meat and replace it in the oven. Do not re-cover, but instead allow the liquid to boil down until your meat browns in its own juices. Following this method, you must keep turning the meat with a long fork so that it gets well-browned on all sides. Sprinkle on more flour if you want a delicious, rich, thick gravy, and gradually add a few more tablespoons of water. Finally return your vegetables to the oven so that they will be heated. But don't let them overcook. Every variety of meat, fish, and game can be cooked in a Dutch oven. It may be used equally satisfactorily over grill, portable grill, or pit.

Various kinds of corn bread may likewise be baked in the Dutch oven. Just grease the oven's bottom and sides thoroughly with bacon fat or shortening, pour in your batter, cover, and set on hot embers. Then pile more hot embers on the oven's top and sides, and in half an hour your bread will be done to a temptingly golden hue.

Also use the Dutch oven for steaming clams and other shellfish. First scrub the shells carefully and put in the oven. Then add a very little water, cover closely and place over the fire or grill.

The Chinese Oven

Among the stationary brick-built fireplaces now becoming more and more popular on the West Coast is the Chinese oven. This is a modern adaptation of equipment used in China as far back as the Han Dynasty (206 B.C. to 20 A.D.).

The Chinese oven consists of four brick walls approximately four feet in height. On top, there is a lid with damper arrangement for regulating the size and intensity of the fire below. In this, the Chinese oven offers a distinct advantage, in that it provides exactly the degree of heat required for every cooking purpose. Further, there is ample accomodation for large-scale cooking, which of course appeals to barbecue addicts who often entertain huge crowds. In cooking racks of lamb, steaks, chicken, and squab, you first kindle a fast fire in the oven so as to heat the bricks thoroughly. When this is done, you push your fire beneath the plate warmer in the rear, using a hoe for this task. Then, by merely opening the oven door, you create a draft which

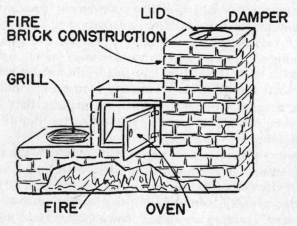

sends the heat upward with great speed and intensity. You regulate this with the damper, using a very hot fire in cooking steaks, fowl, and the like, and, by the same token, a diminished fire for roasting other meats. Steaks nearest the fire naturally brown more quickly and must be rotated accordingly to insure proper browning on both sides. Meats cooked in the Chinese oven style look appetizing and have a very delectable wood-smoke flavor. A prime roast of beef cooks at a temperature of about 300 degrees F., with the damper half open, in three or four hours (according to its size), and reveals a nicely browned outer coating, with an inside pinkish in color, yet nicely cooked.

With a Chinese oven, you can begin cooking almost immediately. There's no waiting for your fire to burn down to coals.

Essential Working Tools

Below are the tools you'll need if you intend to go in for complete barbecue cookery. Here we list everything you *should* have. You can start off your career as an outdoor chef, however, with a few of the most essential ones and add more later on, if you like. If you are already an expert, you'll no doubt have these and more—and you will agree that all are mighty handy for their specific uses. If you are a beginner, your having them will quicken your ascent to stardom in this fascinating realm of culinary artistry.

First, you should have a wooden-handled steel spatula, long enough to permit you to work always far enough from the heat to be comfortable. The blade should be wide and pliable so it can slip easily between food and griddle. You will use a spatula quite frequently in grilling ham, bacon, sausages, eggs, and, of course, hot cakes for family breakfasts or company "brunches."

Second, you need a long-armed fork to match the spatula.

Third, a pair of double-wire broilers with long handles of standard size for steaks, chops, split fowl and fish.

Fourth, at least two different-sized frying pans, skillets, or "spiders" (as they are called Down East). Make sure that your larger one is a hefty steel fry pan from 16½ to 21 inches across, 2¾ inches deep, and having a 20½-inch handle (again for cooler and more comfortable fireside cooking). In the large pan you will easily be able to pan-fry four steaks or chickens or as many as a dozen hamburgers at a time. Also plenty of ham and eggs. And one 12-inch regular cast-iron job for ordinary use.

Fifth, barbecue gloves and a good serviceable professional chef's apron and cap. Wives, girl friends, and guests as a rule look after the supplying of these accessories, and if you rate with them the way most barbecue chefs do, it won't be necessary to buy these.

Sixth, a serviceable oaken carving board, or, if you are really ambitious and intend to go into this barbecuing business with both feet—as we hope you will—a small butcher's block. The latter not only may be very useful in the matter of cutting up meats, but will serve you well in chopping up onions and other vegetables—even in salad-making. Provided, of course, you always keep it immaculately sanded and cleaned.

Seventh, a huge salad bowl (about 20 inches in diameter) such as home economists and housewives rely upon for the preparation of everything from salads to fruits. You'll also find this handy for serving a mess of baked potatoes. For kneading homemade bread and biscuits, too, if you venture into this highly worthwhile culinary activity.

Eighth, a supply of 12-inch wooden plates for serving guests—a few more than the number of persons you ever expect to entertain. Food is so primitively satisfying when served on wooden dishes, and they won't dull your best steak knives, either.

Ninth, a supply of rustproof stainless steel knife, fork, and spoon sets.

Tenth, of course you must have at least twelve or more sturdy steak knives with blades of stainless steel and aluminum or wooden handles! Beautiful, efficient sets come in a case and will last you a lifetime.

Eleventh, a full set of top-grade working knives:
>   a. a slender, sharp knife for roasts
>   b. a versatile French knife for various purposes
>   c. a heavy-duty carving knife and fork
>   d. a butcher's cleaver
>   e. a meat saw

Twelfth, a carborundum or steel knife sharpener.

Thirteenth, large salt and pepper grinders. The true epicure uses only fresh-ground pepper and salt in preparing foods.

Fourteenth, plenty of towels—preferably paper, encased in a weatherproof rack for hanging close to your work table. You will discover their usefulness in draining meats and vegetables as well as their normal purpose of drying hands and wiping grill and table surfaces from time to time.

Fifteenth, a chuck box which you can make yourself to fit into the rear compartment of your car or station wagon in case you need it later, away from home. This should be spacious enough to hold the following:

salt and pepper grinders

Charcrust (a unique flavoring compound available at all gourmet shops like The Epicure's Mart in Greenwich, Connecticut)

seasoned salt

herbs, spices, vinegars (tarragon for seafood; garlic for steaks, roasts, etc.; mixed herbs for salad dressings, marinades, etc.)

marinating sauce

sugar (both brown and white)

mustard and curry

tea, coffee

Worcestershire and Tabasco sauces

basting brush—a *"must"* for all barbecuing!

charcoal—keep in an enclosed can or bag—dry. Briquets are best.

Charcolite. This is the best way to start your fire; kerosene and gasoline are both dangerous and give off unpleasant odors so harmful to delicate foods!

soap—both cake and powder

cleansing powder

portable grill

chef's apron and cap

skewers

Sixteenth, tray boy, which is the portable arrangement referred to in all our recipes later on in this book. On it you will place your cooking essentials before beginning to barbecue. There are large square oak planks on the market which will serve this purpose.

Seventeenth, a large metal coffee pot, percolator, or glass coffee maker.

Eighteenth, a Thermos container capable of holding from one to five gallons of cold or hot food and drinks.

Nineteenth, an ice bucket.

Twentieth, an enclosed garbage-disposal unit or heavy-paper sanitary bags. Make sure they are of the enclosed type to minimize the invasion of flies and insects and to prevent unsavory odors.

Do's and Don'ts Every Barbecuer Should Observe

Do—

1. Locate your fireplace in the direction of the prevailing winds. This insures a more efficient draft and carries away smoke from the front of the fireplace—and the faces of guests.

2. Make certain the bottom of your firebox is high enough to give you a convenient cooking surface at a working level commensurate with your height and cooking posture.

3. Cover the top of your fireplace walls with flat stones or sheet metal to serve as a work-surface ledge and to prevent water from seeping between the stone or fire-brick inner lining and the outside masonry.

4. Build an adequate foundation *beneath* your fireplace, well below the freezing depth of the soil. This is very important in cold regions—it will prevent damage to your pit or grill.

5. Pave at least three feet around and in front of your fireplace for added fire safety and as a protection against weather and foot traffic. Use bricks, flagstones, or concrete to harmonize with your other surroundings.

6. Protect outer stonework with a heat-resisting lining of

fire brick inside the firebox and other areas that come into contact with flame or heat.

7. Use mortar composed of 75 per cent fire clay and 25 per cent Portland cement. Spread thinly for a 1/16-inch joint in laying fire bricks.

8. Allow room for expansion and contraction of metal parts to prevent cracks and other damaging results of heat and cold to fireplace stonework.

DON'T—

1. *Ever* use kerosene, gasoline or greases of any kind in kindling your fire! We emphasize this point once again, because these fire starters, besides being dangerous, mar the flavors of foods. Briquets made from the hard woods of Northern Michigan are the perfect barbecue fuel. They require a little more time in becoming fully lighted, but once under way they give you a uniform, radiant heat for all barbecue methods of cookery. Regular charcoal may be used, however, though you should obtain the two-inch lumps if at all possible. But try to cook always with briquets if you want that delicious taste coat to meats that makes avid trenchermen of all who sample your handiwork. If you use wood select only the hard woods—hickory, oak, prune, or apple wood—but positively no resinous woods like pine, cedar, and fir. These will only spit, flare, and burn away in no time, and you simply cannot depend upon them for good, hot, even-glowing coals.

2. *Never* cook over the flame or in a thick smoke. Wait until your fuel is down to a mass of radiant embers. Remember that roasting especially is best done at a temperature around 300 degrees F. Keep at hand a bulb sprinkler to take down your flames whenever necessary.

3. *Never* forget to extinguish your fire completely once the party is over or before you leave your grill for the night. But do not douse your fire with water. If you do, you risk freezing and cracking the mortar, bricks, or stones.

4. *Never* waste the charcoal or wood ashes after cleaning out the tray underneath the firebox. These are excellent for

growing vegetables and other plants. Maintain a suitable storage bin nearby for ashes. Being a barbecue enthusiast, you'll very likely keep a garden and will know all about this, anyway.

5. *Never* forget to baste all roasts—game, fowl, or fish—frequently with marinade sauces and pan drippings.

6. *Never* allow anyone else to do the main part of the cooking. Do this yourself. Appoint assistants, if you wish, from among your pals who know *how* to barbecue. It's trite but true—too many cooks spoil a barbecue! For your own protection, you'd better invite them to read through these Do's and Don'ts before allowing them to wield a skillet.

7. *Never* forget your timing. This is most important if you wish to insure that all dishes reach the table at exactly the right time—when *hot*. Prepare salads and soups, if you plan to have them, in advance. Let vegetables bake or boil during the period when you broil your meats.

8. *Never* leave anything to chance. Plan your entire meal ahead of time. Have all foods and equipment immediately at hand once you begin to cook.

Still More Pointers

Here are a few pointers to insure your becoming an adept barbecue hand under all conditions of bachelor freedom or apron-string servitude.

A. Meat: In buying beef, always seek your butcher's advice. He will tell you if it is well hung. One of the secrets of a good steak is its age. The longer it hangs in the meat market the better it is; four weeks is ideal. Good beef has an open grain and the fat in a young steer is of a crumbling or oily smoothness, except, of course, in the brisket, neck, or other fibrous pieces. The lean should be of an appealing carnation-red color, the fat white—not yellow. Top-grade beef will be well-marbled, with tiny streaks of fat all through the lean. Ask your butcher for extra suet for use in rubbing your grill or broiling rack well before beginning to cook.

B. The grades are: U. S. Prime, which is the top grade or finest; U. S. Choice, an excellent meat you can buy with confidence; U. S. Good, entirely acceptable if well hung or aged. If possible, you should order all meats far enough in advance to insure their being aged for at least two or three weeks. Remove steaks from the refrigerator two hours before broiling.

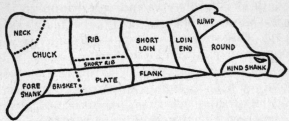

C. It will pay you to familiarize yourself with the above chart which shows a carcass of beef sectioned according to the nomenclature under which it is sold. That choice upper part of the beef, just back of the porterhouse or short loin section, you will recognize as the sirloin from which those zesty favorites of all men derive. A double sirloin is known as a baron of beef. And by way of a conversational piece to dish out along with your cooking, we give you a little of the history of the word "sirloin."

Merry Charles II, many-wived Henry VIII, and James I of Bible fame are all reputed to have had something to do with the christening of the noble sirloin cut of beef. According to legend, one of these royal gentlemen—probably in his cups—pulled out his sword and knighted a huge beef before a banquet: Sir Loin! According to those who have been more careful in their research, the "sir" of sirloin is believed to be a corruption of the French word "sur"—*on* or *upon*. "*Sur*" joins itself to the French word "*longe*" for loin. Take your choice of either origin, but there is one thing you can always be sure of—the sirloin steak is surely worthy of any king who will ever grace your patio table!

D. Pounding steaks with a cleaver is sometimes good for breaking down their tissues. Deep freezing also does wonders for all meats. Rubbing with a damp cloth—but never washing under water—is likewise advisable. If you like garlic, make three or four incisions in the steak and insert a quarter clove of garlic in each incision so that the garlic can be seen when cooked and then removed before serving. To most amateur chefs, particularly those who go in for barbecuing, *no* garlic is sacrilegious—*too much* a capital crime!

E. A generous coat of oil plus seasonings and slow cooking, and you've done about everything possible for a steak, if you like it unadorned—except, of course, buying wisely in the first place.

F. Some gourmets like filets of the steaks, some prefer the bone—medium rare, well done or charred. Whatever their choice, you can suit their preferences to a "t" when you barbecue, that's for sure! Especially if you use marinades for tenderizing the meats and for piquant delicacy of flavor.

G. Steaks, fish, game, and fowl are more delectable when accompanied by something crunchy and fresh-flavored like cucumber sticks, tiny carrots, celery, radishes, scallions and olives. Cabbage well-crisped in ice water before shredding may be whipped into a delicious cole slaw that makes a worthy complement of such Olympian fare.

H. As we previously mentioned, your grill or broiling rack should be rubbed with beef fat or suet before barbecuing steaks. Allow one pound for each healthy, steak-loving adult. Sirloin leads in popularity, but both porterhouse and T-bone have their followers. Never take your steak from the refrigerator and throw it on the fire—give it at least one hour in room temperature before grilling.

Cook a thick steak ($2\frac{1}{2}$ inches is the best thickness) at moderate heat about six inches above your bed of embers. Season well with coarse salt and freshly ground pepper, and when nicely browned on one side turn carefully, using tongs and a spatula instead of a fork to avoid puncturing the seared meat. Broil other side.

Remember that a little showmanship goes a long way. Have your audience assembled for that thrilling moment when you remove the steak from the fire to test the color. Cut a small incision near the bone to be sure that the inside is rare but not raw. If meat looks purple, return it to the fire until the correct state of doneness is achieved.

A good steak deserves a fitting entrance. Serve it forth on a sizzling hot platter or a wooden carving board that has been preheated. Mushrooms broiled in butter or crisp French-fried onions make an appetizing and delicious crown for this king of foods.

Remember that nothing is worse than chilled meat, so serve it quickly the minute it is done.

I. Pan-broil steaks less than two inches thick, unless you are an expert! To pan-broil, use a large steel, iron or copper pan or a flat-topped griddle which fits over your grill. Grease with beef fat or suet, and when it is smoking hot, pan-broil steak quickly, seasoning with salt and pepper (fresh-ground) to taste, turning steaks constantly. If steak sticks to the metal, lubricate your pan again with more fat or suet. Steak is apt to cook more rapidly this way, so keep an eagle eye on it.

J. Thin minute steaks, cube steaks, or tenderloin slices are marvelous pan-broiled and served on toasted bread or rolls as steak sandwiches. (See recipe, page 72.)

K. Another pointer well worth keeping in mind is to have your butcher lard a whole tenderloin of beef with one-fourth inch strips of salt pork and wrap with thin strips of beef suet. You then fasten your beef to a spit and broil over coals, turning meat every half hour so that all sides are evenly browned.

L. As for chopped meat, see recipes, pages 84-87.

Don't be Just a Steak Man

Vary your menus from sirloin to lamb chops, mutton, venison, charcoal-broiled chicken, spare-ribs—even to Long Island duckling, which may be broiled in the same way as chicken, though it requires *twice as long*.

Whatever you do, don't be a stickler for culinary convention. Be ambidextrous with your entrees—juggle them about with abandon! For example, a good old English roast beef goes well with almost anything—a Chinese dish, a

Hawaiian salad, even a typically American dessert. Use your imagination. Then you will be famous far and wide as a barbecue chef *par excellence!*

Why not even tackle roasting a whole baby pig or baby lamb weighing from eight to 20 pounds? To do this, first split down the chin bone from inside, being careful not to cut its outer skin. Remove shoulder bones and replace them with wooden sticks. Rub barbecue sauce (with a catsup base) into cavities. After pig has cooked thirty minutes, puncture the skin with an ice pick to allow more fat to escape. Cook about 35 minutes per pound, but be positive that your meat is well-done!

Meals planned with chicken as a main entree are always fine eating, healthful, and a joy to cook. Chicken is ever a leading department of barbecue cheffery, and you should get right into it almost as soon as your barbecue pit or grill is built.

Young chickens or broilers weighing from two to five pounds are ideal for barbecuing. Have birds split in half, then remove back and breastbones. Use game shears or a knife with a curved blade for this.

Chickens are brushed with oil or fat, salted, peppered, and then hung on wire or skewered on a spit. Squabs are cooked the same way. They require approximately twenty minutes.

We are all enthusiastically fond of chicken, barbecued, broiled, fried, or roasted. Until recent years, however, this favorite was mostly restricted to a few months of the year. Now in most sections of America we have the *broiler-fryer*— a bird developed solely for meat purposes that is more tender, more flavorable, meatier, and available all year 'round. The *broiler-fryer* comes ready to cook in sizes from two pounds and up.

In barbecuing ducks, first be sure to clean and wash thoroughly, preferably in water to which honey has been added. Dry in the open air, then tie vent to the neck and stuff with poultry dressing through the neck opening to fill cavity. Cook one and a half hours or longer until done to taste. In this process, the duck swells slightly, its meat is tenderized, and it has a golden-brown outer surface when done, as a result of using the honey.

Wild duck and geese should be rubbed with soya sauce or your own favorite marinade. They require approximately 2½ hours at 250 degrees F.; longer if stuffed.

Shashlik is probably the first name broiled meat ever had, being the word the Russians have given to a Georgian way of preparing lamb—only the Georgians call it "m'tswade." Our friend Prometheus, who stole fire from heaven, is supposed to have brought it to the Caucasus, and it was there on Mt. Kazbek, or Caucasus, that he was chained by Zeus for punishment. Shashlik, being originally a dish for hunters, is seldom made from beef. Unless larded, the latter is too dry for broiling in cubes over embers. On the other hand, a leg of pork is too fat, though it is sometimes used when lamb is unavailable. Get a nice leg of lamb from five to seven pounds in weight. Then consult our recipe (page 165).

The Persians and Armenians broil cubed meat spitted with vegetables and call it shish kebab. Broiled lamb they term lulu kebab. But any way you cook them, shish kebabs are lulus to serve at a barbecue fiesta. They are highly satisfying to the taste, and they create an opportunity for the showmanship that means so much to the enjoyment of a barbecue party. Many of our G.I.'s discovered shish kebabs in India under the name "seekh kebob," or as "sasaties" in the Union of South Africa and "sates" in the Dutch East Indies. These "sates," "sasaties," or "shish kebabs" (as most people know them) are frequently prepared with pork, beef, veal, or even mutton. Whether spitted on a sword (as they were in the beginning) or on a branch of hazel wood, kebabs are delicately seasoned yet hearty meats, and offer unlimited scope for the fanciful play of the barbecue chef's imagination. On page 164 you will find a sample recipe to test your skill.

Some Easy Steps

Perhaps one thing, more than any other, has made barbecue fans of men who like to cook. That is the fact that you can cook and serve a dinner for a dozen or more persons and have a perfectly wonderful time doing it. It's no trick at all if you take the following steps.

First of all, prepare your salad. Have a big wooden bowl heaped with crisp mixed greens, red-ripe tomatoes, slices of cucumbers, and slivers of anchovies laced with a tangy dressing at the last minute. Besides this, have plates, linen, knives, forks, etc. set out buffet-style on a snack bar.

Keep a hefty supply of man-sized Maine or Idaho potatoes, nicely oiled and browned, on one side of your grill or in your warming oven. The same goes for other vegetables or side dishes.

Have plenty of coffee, drinks—soft and hard—and water convenient enough for your guests to help themselves.

If you are still a novice, stick for awhile to the eternal male triangle of steak, potatoes, and pie—a combination which, we promise you, will make any man other than a dyspeptic drool with anticipation. But do follow our earlier advice and venture out just as soon as you possibly can into wider horizons of outdoor cuisine. Barbecue *all* kinds of meats! Don't just be a *steak* man. Anyone can be that.

Speaking of potatoes—besides baking or boiling, try mashing them with zucchini or squash, topped with whipped cream and grated cheese daubed on with an opulent hand. That'll make 'em let out their belts for sure!

And pardon us, please, if we dwell a moment on the matter of boiling potatoes. Potatoes are allergic to huge vats of water—cold, lukewarm, or mildly boiling. Potatoes should be covered with water that is bubbling at a rolling boil. Boiling should be continuous; otherwise you will get water-logged potatoes, particularly if you use too much water instead of merely covering the spuds. Furthermore, if not removed from the water immediately when done, potatoes will crack. If (though we hope not!) your potatoes are suffering from senility due to being around in storage too long, you can revive them by bathing in ice-cold water awhile before cooking. Then they require the same treatment as new ones.

Pies and Homemade Breads *

Look over our pie recipe on page 284 and you will see that it is easily within your culinary capabilities. There are splendid ready-mixed pie crusts on the market, if you do not want to bother to make your own. However, if you do make your own crust, mix and roll it on waxed paper. Then cover with a second sheet of waxed paper. Roll and chill thoroughly before lining your pie plate. Brush lower crust with egg white beaten with a teaspoon of cold water. This prevents soggy lower crust. Before baking, brush top crust with cream and sprinkle lightly with sugar. Then brush top crust once again with melted butter about five minutes before taking pie from the oven. *Man*—can't you just smell that pie you'll soon be cooking!

Oh, yes, and while you are in this gustatory trance, may we also suggest that you try your masculine skill at bread-baking? If you're a bit skittish, first experiment with the prepared mixes. But if you really want to become a master chef, say to hell with ready mixes and pallid, tasteless, rubbery store bread itself, with its much-touted restored vitamins. Bake your own! Yessiree! And honestly, you can do it as easily as rolling out a pie crust—which we also assure you is a cinch. Tender, flaky biscuits or feathery-light muffins that break open still fragrantly steaming, chock full of berries, dates, or nuts, and fairly running with butter! Or yummy old-fashioned corn bread! These are really toothsome and delicious! They're epicurean food that any barbecue gourmet may well take pride in preparing and serving. You can bake them while a casserole is browning inside your oven or while the potatoes are baking. Or use your Dutch oven as we told you on page 14. See our bread recipes on pages 270-277 for actual details.

Tray Boy

Your tray becomes your lackey in barbecue technique. Check the ingredients of your Tray Boy to be sure you have in-

---

* Pie-baking is restricted to barbecue units with ovens only.

cluded all you need and to save additional trips to the kitchen. Add any extras your own original version of the recipe may require.

Tips at Random

Soya sauce or kitchen bouquet brushed on meats gives a beautiful crisp brown glaze and a delicious salty flavor. Particularly good for steaks, chicken, lamb, veal, and fish. Use a glass or enamel pan only. Never aluminum!

Honey also creates a good rich glaze on barbecued foods and is marvelous on chicken.

To reduce the heat under a skillet or pan, use an asbestos pad.

Quick-frozen vegetables are excellent for outdoor food preparation, as they are compact, easy and quick to cook.

Beyond what we have already told you about barbecuing, its history and philosophy, kinds of permanent and portable equipment, our Do's and Don'ts, and the general information regarding meats and the preparation of a few typical barbecue meals, you need only the recipes that follow. All have been carefully, lovingly culled from hundreds of savory dishes that it has been our happy good fortune to collect over many years.

Cook on, hearty members of our friendly clan! And may you and your lucky friends who sample your wares ever live longer and more happily for it!

FOUR EASY-TO-BUILD FIREPLACES
WITH READY-BUILT UNITS

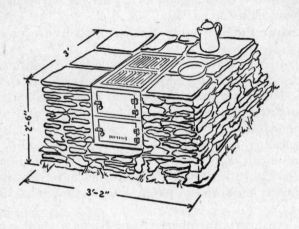

1. Estimated number of materials you'll need:

Stone and Brick

20 cu. ft. stone or 350 common bricks
50 fire bricks
2 sacks cement mortar
¼ cu. yd. sand

Cement Block

25 cement blocks 8x8x16″
20 cement blocks 4x8x16″
50 fire bricks
1 sack cement
⅛ cu. yd. sand

Material listed is above ground. Foundation not included. Be sure foundation is below frost level. 4-inch foundation pad requires 3½ cu. ft. concrete. 6-inch foundation pad requires 5¼ cu. ft. concrete. Ask your local builders' supply about your requirements.

2. Estimated number of materials:

Stone and Brick	**Cement Block**
35 cu. ft. stone or 600 common bricks	30 cement blocks 8x8x16″
50 fire bricks	50 cement blocks 4x8x16″
3 sacks cement mortar	25 fire bricks
⅜ cu. yd. sand	1½ sacks cement mortar
	¼ cu. yd. sand

Material listed is above ground. Foundation not included. Be sure foundation is below frost level. 4-inch foundation pad requires 4 cu. ft. concrete. 6-inch foundation pad requires 6 cu. ft. concrete. Ask your local builder's supply about your requirements.

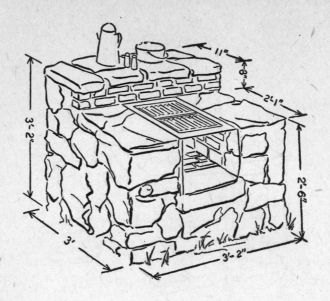

3. Estimated number of materials:

Stone and Brick

25 cu. ft. stone or 450 common
  bricks
25 fire bricks
3 sacks cement mortar
½ cu. yd. sand

Cement Block

30 cement blocks 8x8x16″
25 cement blocks 4x8x16″
25 fire bricks
1½ sack cement mortar
¼ cu. yd. sand

Material listed is above ground. Foundation not included. Be sure foundation is below frost level. 4-inch foundation pad requires 3½ cu. ft. concrete. 6-inch foundation pad requires 5¼ cu. ft. concrete. Ask your local builders about your requirements.

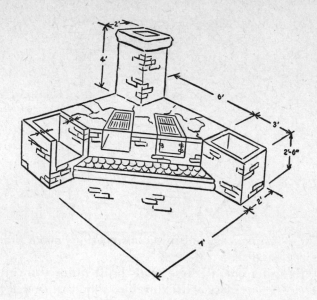

4. Estimated number of materials:

<table>
<tr><td>**Stone and Brick**</td><td>**Cement Block**</td></tr>
<tr><td>225 cu. ft. stone or 4000 common bricks</td><td>200 cement blocks 8x8x16"
350 cement blocks 4x8x16"</td></tr>
<tr><td>50 fire bricks</td><td>50 fire bricks</td></tr>
<tr><td>24 sacks cement mortar</td><td>12 sacks cement mortar</td></tr>
<tr><td>4 cu. yd. sand</td><td>2 cu. yd. sand</td></tr>
</table>

Material listed is above ground. Foundation not included. 6-inch foundation requires 1 cubic yard concrete. Be sure foundation is below frost level.

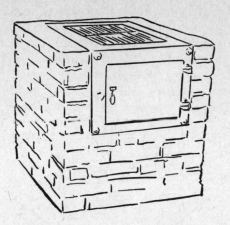

5a. These simple, easy-to-build constructions make practical, efficient fireplaces.

By using one of these ready-built units, you can have a long-lasting fireplace with durable, solid-cast-iron fixtures.

5b. A popular de luxe unit that comes to you ready to set right onto your flat fireplace foundation. Just stack your building material around it. Heavy all-cast-iron doors and solid grill-top assembly. Has an additional ash-pit door and frame. The sturdy, rolled-iron supporting frame makes building your masonry a simple task. It contains an additional built-in charcoal-fire level to which the fire grates can be transferred when desired. Here you have a long-lasting outdoor fireplace about as complete and elegant as you would want.

6. Iron frame, iron doors (lower one has draft regulator), and grates are the "works" of this unit. Lower grate, in two sections, can be placed at either of two levels to burn charcoal or wood. Top has grate for meats and a solid grid for rolls and the like; about $21.00. Installed as here illustrated, it needs no chimney, but has adjoining storage cupboards for dishes, utensils and fuel, and also a wide counter top.

7. Both brick fireplace, a ready-made grill, and an oven are here included. The Fryo-Grill unit has steel sides, and a back with flue connections in case you want a chimney to carry off smoke and insure better draft. The grate can be moved up or down to burn charcoal or wood, and the

steel steak grill is removable. The whole unit (21½ inches long, 17 inches wide, 22 inches high) can be removed in winter. About $25.00.

Separate oven and grill are included in the steel form beneath. Baking oven is the half-round compartment. Wood, coal, or charcoal can be burned. Grates are adjustable with baffles to control draft, heat and smoke direction. Built-in flue section is ready for chimney construction. About $40.00. Steel cabinets built beside unit provide ample storage.

8. A basic grill in two sections with accompanying solid-fitting grill frame makes an ideal yet simple outdoor fireplace. Construction can be cast-iron with grill bars flat on top, and a tapered underside for maximum heat efficiency. Fit frame square in whatever masonry you build to hold it and have a recessed flange running completely around inside area to receive each grill. Bolts can be imbedded to anchor whole unit as snugly as part of your brick or stone.

Plan for more style than a regular fireplace. You can allow for a draft-control door on your firebox, securely attached by sturdy pin-hinge flanges to a snug-fitting frame that is bolted to your fireplace structure. Made of heavy duty cast-iron, both of these additional sections (door and frame) come ready for attachment to your masonry.

A compact, solid unit comes with grills and doors attached that you build your masonry up to and around with chimney in back. Comes ready for instant assembly and insertion into your masonry. All parts are cast iron on a rolled-iron frame. Unit includes a second fire level to which firebox grids transfer for instant-firing charcoal, a bottom draft-control and ash pit door, the regular heatproof door handles and grill handler. About $33.00.

9. This compact patio grill, with two motor-turned spits, gives you a barbecue anywhere. Motor is electrically driven

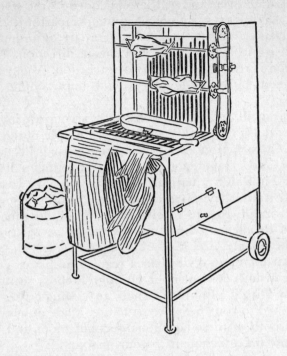

—simply plug it in and relax. The vertical and horizontal grills should please the most exacting barbecue chef. A drip-pan is also included, to catch drippings and hold basting sauce.

"Woodland" folding grill of aluminized steel folds flat.
Around $6.00.

10. A portable that's easily assembled or knocked-down . . .
can be taken anywhere.

Sturdy, lightweight construction, makes Broil-Air an ideal traveller. Packing carton takes little space in any auto trunk—and it assembles complete, "ready-for-fire" in five minutes. Rubber-tired wheels and perfect balance make it easy to move anywhere, any time.

Charcoal, wood or other fuel instantly ignited by use of the blower. Fire brought to intense heat in three minutes. Two or three inch deep bed of glowing coals. Life-time, all-steel construction. Steel utility tray below hearth and braced shelf is standard equipment.

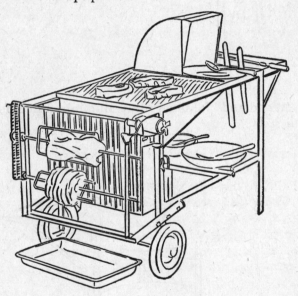

11. Electrically Driven. No hand turning or standing over a hot fire. Simply load one or both skewers, start motor and join your friends while your roast or fowl takes on a golden brown hue, sending tingling cooking aromas in every direction.

Both vertical and horizontal barbecuing with the freedom of automatic cooking.

12a. Folding model that is portable . . . quick to set up . . .
rigid.

This Master grill opens in a jiffy and, in camp stool
fashion, stands firm anywhere—on grass, sand or rocky ground.
This model features V-shaped fire trough with reinforcing
draft-channels, designed for correct, slow burning, steady
heat . . . stout, permanently attached legs . . . heavy sheet
steel construction throughout . . . weather-resistant aluminum
finish.

This model broils as well as barbecues. Removable barbecue spit for sizzling roasts—juicy chunks of meat: broil as
many as 24 hamburgers on wire grid. Windshield conserves
heat, shelters fire, keeps food warm. New warming shelf for
extra capacity. Packed in individual, permanent, carrying
carton with handle.

New patented charcoal grate, hinged to grill, improves
draft; slows fire to best broiling heat. Charcoal grate.

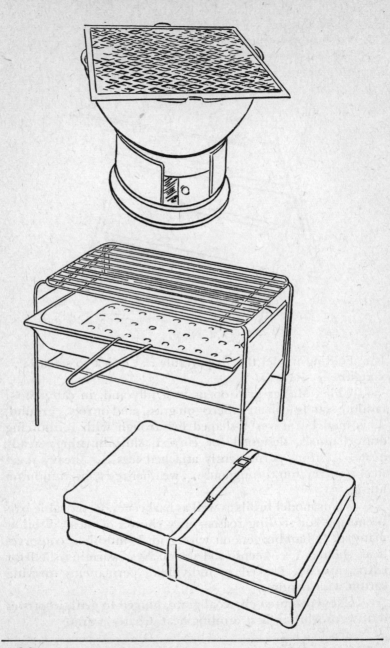

On opposite page:

12b. Caribbean firepot made of aluminum, weighs 8½ lbs. is 12″ across, 9″ high. With grill. About $25.00.

12c. A "Hi-Low" Folding Grill with tray that adjusts to four levels, has fiber carrying case, weighs 12 lbs. About $7.

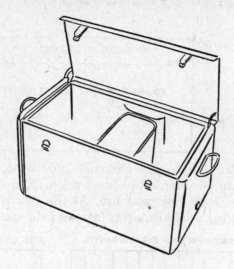

12d. Handy portable refrigerator, the Thermaster. About $11.00.

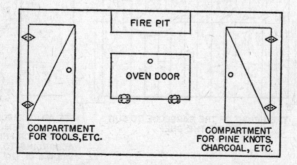

12e. (1) Built-in compartments, one for tools and one for fuel are an excellent feature of this compact barbecue which has an oven door below the fire pit.

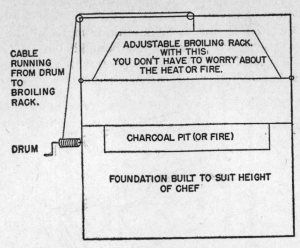

CABLE RUNNING FROM DRUM TO BROILING RACK.

ADJUSTABLE BROILING RACK. WITH THIS, YOU DON'T HAVE TO WORRY ABOUT THE HEAT OR FIRE.

DRUM

CHARCOAL PIT (OR FIRE)

FOUNDATION BUILT TO SUIT HEIGHT OF CHEF

(2) When guests pile charcoal, pine knots or any fuel on the fire, an adjustable broiling rack will insure the chef of control over his heat and fire. As the sketch shows, this arrangement has a definite advantage over the stationary rack.

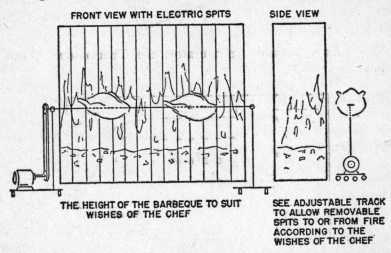

FRONT VIEW WITH ELECTRIC SPITS

SIDE VIEW

THE HEIGHT OF THE BARBEQUE TO SUIT WISHES OF THE CHEF

SEE ADJUSTABLE TRACK TO ALLOW REMOVABLE SPITS TO OR FROM FIRE ACCORDING TO THE WISHES OF THE CHEF

(3) Another way of controlling the heat from the fire —placing the spits on a movable track allows the chef to regulate the heat from a vertical grill to his own satisfaction.

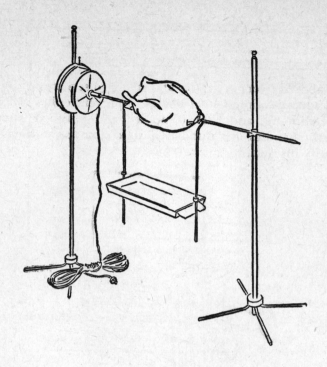

13a. No tedious hand turning with this electric spit.

Turns load up to 50 lbs. when properly balanced, three times a minute.

Standard equipment includes two sets of uprights—one set 48″, and one set 24″ long—and two sets of pan holders. Drip pan is not furnished. Steel spit is 46″ long.

Each unit is packed in three convenient shipping cartons. Assembled in a few minutes. Shipping Weight 35 lbs. About $40.00.

13b. Kabob skewers in deluxe and standard sets are 32″ long, have square stainless steel blades to prevent cubes of food from slipping, and the 10″ waxed and polished square wooden handles are numbered to enable each diner to identify his own.

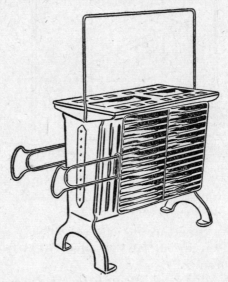

14. Here's an inexpensive, compact, portable and convenient vertical broiler that broils rapidly on both sides of the fuel basket. Meat is basted while it is broiling and all fats are eliminated. Wire grills are reversible. A second basting may be given by merely turning the wire grill. One person can readily handle four Broiloasters set up in a row. Two wire grills can always be on the fire while the other two are being emptied and refilled.

　　May be used anywhere. Needs no connection. Take it on your outing or picnic, use it at home, in garage, cellar, or porch. Costs about $14.00. Extra wire grills $2.80 a pair.

15. This new charcoal broiler is designed to bring out the best in steaks, chops or any meat. Sturdy, durable and practical.

Diameter of top grid is 13¼″, height 9″, weight 25 lbs. It is easily moved—can be used anywhere without connection. No fuss—no mess—no trouble at all . . .

A small amount of charcoal briquets (a 2 or 3″ layer) will broil steaks, chops, hamburgers, fish or game with that delicious flavor that only charcoal imparts. Intense heat sears meat, thus retaining juice and flavor. Price about $15.00. Charcoal Briquets come in convenient paper bags.

16a. 21 inch, bigger-than-life-size skillet to fry hamburgers, hash-browns, etc. Pan is easy-cleaning, polished steel, with a long cast-iron handle to keep hands cool. About $12.00.

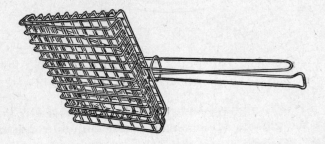

16b. Mammoth broiler. It opens to hold three young chickens to be turned often for that all-over crackly brown.

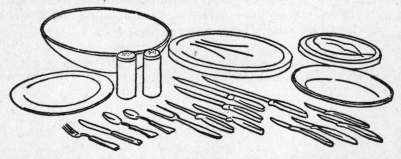

16c. Shown above is an oval-shaped trencher in natural-finish wood. At right, two oak planks, one big enough to serve five or six, the other for individual service. Both are kiln-dried wood and have wells to catch meat juices. The round platter is for cooking on, as well as eating off'n. Also, a 4-piece stainless steel cutlery set with handsome handles of brass or copper. At fine shops throughout the country. And just below: A two-pronged fork and five matching knives. The four individual steak knives at the extreme right of the same sketch are sharp steel.

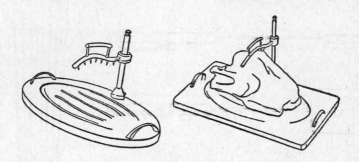

16d. Here is a piece of equipment we highly recommend to the well-experienced barbecue fan who wishes to serve with the greatest finesse. This Carv-King holds the meat or fowl securely in place and enables one to carve slices as thick or thin as desired. The cutting is done against a wood surface at an angle most convenient to the carver. The clamping arm may be locked in three different positions so any part of the meat or fowl can be exposed and it can be raised or lowered to accommodate meat of any thickness. May be easily dismantled for quick cleaning and assembled in a matter of seconds. Available at better stores in several sizes and shapes from $27.00.

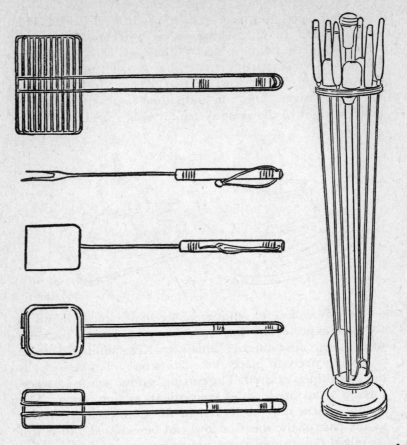

17a. *Right*. Handsome barbecue tools are easy to carry to and from fire in handy rack. Wooden salt, pepper, and spice shakers fit in slots next to handles in upper part of rack.

17b. *Left*. These gay, sturdy barbecue tools are inexpensive. Roasting rack broils a big, juicy steak; fork handy for turning food. Giant spatula an expert hamburger turner. Hinged grill broils hamburgers. The smaller roaster rack cooks hot dogs.

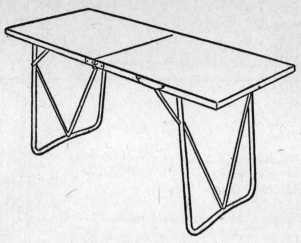

18. Folds to fit in a car.
   Opens to feed an army.
   The Foldaway weighs 19 pounds yet holds 50 times its own weight. It is easily carried, stored; the answer to all barbecue problems. Sets up in a jiffy. A lot of table for a little money.

WINE CHART

Aperitifs:

> Dry Sherry
> Vermouths
> Madeira (Gloria Mundi)

Table wines that go well with meat:

> Claret
> Burgundy
> Zinfandel
> Chianti

Table wines that go well with fish and fowl:

> Sauterne
> Rhine wine
> Chablis

Dessert and after-dinner wines:

> Muscatel
> Port
> Tokay
> Madeira of the heavy-bodied and richer types (see your
> wine dealer)

Sparkling all-purpose wines that may be served any time:

> Champagne
> Sparkling Burgundy

Any of the many carbonated or so-called crackling wines on the market (see your dealer), such as Moselle and Lancer's Vin Rosé.

1.
Drink Suggestions

**Drink Suggestions to Vary with
Your Barbecue Menus and to Add Conviviality
to Your Party**

Glance through this old classic "For Longer Life" to put you
in a relaxed frame of mind and in a mood to mix some good
drinks for your guests.

> *The horse and mule live thirty years
>   and nothing know of wines and beers;
> The goat and sheep at twenty die
>   and never taste of scotch and rye;
> The cow drinks water by the ton
>   and at eighteen is mostly done;
> The dog at fifteen cashs in
>   Without the aid of rum and gin;*

The cat in milk and water soaks
and then in twelve short years it croaks;
The modest, sober, bone-dry hen
lays eggs for nogs, then dies at ten.
All animals are strictly dry,
they sinless live and sinless die,
But sinful, ginful, rum-soaked men
survive for three-score years and ten;
But some of the mighty few
stay pickled till they are ninety-two.

Don't forget that wines and beer too are on the *must list* of every good barbecue host. Lest you forget, we are including directions for the proper wine to be served with different courses. We suggest that guests be asked in advance whether they prefer wine or beer with the main course.

Alabama Fizz (sometimes called The Southside Fizz)

juice of ½ lemon
1 teaspoon fine granulated sugar
1½ oz. dry gin

Shake well with cracked ice and strain into 8-ounce highball glass. Fill with carbonated water and stir. Decorate with two sprigs of mint. Serve with straws.

Aviation Cocktail

1½ oz. dry gin
½ oz. lemon juice
¼ oz. maraschino cordial

Shake with ice and strain into cocktail glass.

Bacardi Cocktail

juice ½ lime
½ teaspoon sugar
dash of grenadine
1 jigger Bacardi Rum

Shake well in finely chipped ice and strain into cocktail glass.

Bahia Cocktail

    1 dash Angostura Bitters
    1 oz. dry vermouth
    1 oz. sherry
    ¼ oz. Pernod

Stir well in cracked ice and strain into cocktail glass. Twist lemon peel over drink.

Bamboo Cocktail

    2 dashes Angostura Bitters
    1½ oz. sherry
    1½ oz. dry vermouth

Stir well in cracked ice, strain into cocktail glass.

Beer with Egg

(an excellent antidote for the chef who has over-indulged the night before)

    1 glass cold beer (½ pint)
    1 egg

Almost fill glass with beer. Add egg. Beat up with fork. This makes a gold-colored bland drink. Yield: 1 portion.

Black Velvet

    ½ champagne (chilled)
    ½ stout (ice-cold)

Pour together simultaneously and slowly in 14-ounce Collins glass.

Bombay Cocktail

    2 dashes Angostura Bitters
    ¾ oz. dry vermouth
    ¾ oz. sweet vermouth
    1½ oz. brandy
    dash of anisette
    2 dashes of curacao

Shake well with ice and strain into cocktail glass.

Bombay Punch

1 pint brandy
1 pint sherry
3 oz. maraschino liqueur
3 oz. orange curacao
2 quarts champagne or carbonated wine
1 quart carbonated water.

Mix in punch bowl with a large block of hard-frozen crystal-clear ice. Garnish well with slices of fresh fruit. Add champagne or carbonated wine last, just before serving. Serve in wine or Delmonico glasses. Serves 12-14 persons.

Brandy Fizz

1 oz. fresh lime juice
1 teaspoon fine granulated sugar
1½ oz. brandy

Shake well with cracked ice, strain into a 10-ounce highball or fizz glass, fill with carbonated water. Stir slightly.

La Citadelle Cocktail (Port-au-Prince, Haiti)

Into a shaker . . .
3 jiggers of gold rum
½ jigger of whiskey
¼ jigger French vermouth
½ jigger of creme de menthe
½ jigger of anisette
½ jigger of gin
½ jigger of creme de cacao
2 whites of eggs
5 jiggers of cream

Add cracked ice, shake, and serve in chilled champagne glasses or large wine glasses. Just before serving sprinkle nutmeg on top. The above is supposed to serve six thirsty people, according to the Haitian bartender.

Cafe Au Kirsch

1 oz. black coffee
1 oz. kirschwasser
1 teaspoon fine granulated sugar
1 egg white

Shake well with cracked ice and strain into a large cocktail glass.

Cuba Libre

Squeeze juice ½ lime in a 10-ounce Collins glass and drop in lime shell. Add 3 cubes of ice, 1½ oz. rum, and fill glass with cola. Serve with a stir rod.

Fish-House Punch

Dissolve in a large punch bowl ¾ pound fine granulated sugar, then add in the order named: 1 quart lemon juice; 2 quarts Jamaica rum; 1 quart brandy; 2 quarts water; 1 wine glass peach brandy. Place a large block crystal-clear, hard-frozen ice in the mixture and allow it to brew for about two hours. Stir occasionally. In winter when ice melts slowly, more water may be used. In summer, less. Serves a crowd. (This famous punch has been enjoyed by countless celebrities, including Washington and Lafayette).

Gin and Tonic

Rub peel of fresh lime or lemon around inside edge of 8-ounce glass. Pour in 1½ ounce dry gin and add two cubes crystal-clear ice. Add thin slice of lime or lemon. Fill glass with Indian quinine water. (This drink originated in the tropics, but is now an international favorite.)

Horse's Neck (with a kick)

Peel the rind of a lemon, spiral fashion, in one piece. Place one edge of the peel over the lip of a 10-ounce Collins glass, allowing the remainder to curl inside the tumbler. Add cubes of crystal-clear ice. Pour in 1½ ounces of gin or whiskey. Fill with ginger ale.

Java Cooler

    3 hearty dashes Angostura Bitters
    juice ½ lime
    1½ oz. dry gin
    1 split of Indian quinine water
    2 cubes crystal-clear ice

Put the ice into a 10-ounce Collins glass. Squeeze in the juice of lime. Add bitters and gin. Fill glass with the Indian quinine water, stir slightly, serve with a stir rod.

Manhattan Cocktail

    1 or 2 dashes Angostura Bitters for each Manhattan cock-
        tail
    ⅔ whiskey
    ⅓ sweet vermouth

Put ingredients in a mixing glass filled with cracked ice, stir until thoroughly mixed, strain and serve.

Martini Cocktail (dry)

    ⅔ dry gin
    ⅓ dry vermouth

Stir in cracked ice, strain into cocktail glass dressed with olive or pearl onions. Twist lemon peel over top.

Mint Julep

Fill a 10-ounce Collins glass with finely crushed ice and place to one side. Strip the leaves from 2 sprigs of fresh mint, place leaves in mixing glass and sprinkle with 1 teaspoonful of granulated sugar. Macerate with muddler until mint flavor is released from leaves. Add splash of seltzer and 3 ounces bourbon whiskey. Stir gently, then strain into the prepared Collins glass over the ice. Work a barspoon up and down in the mixture until the outside of the glass begins to frost. Top with a splash of rum, 2 sprigs of fresh mint and a cherry, and serve with straws. Do not touch the glass with warm hands; use a towel while handling to facilitate frosting.

Mint Tom Collins

    2 oz. Old Mr. Boston mint-flavored gin
    juice ½ lemon
    1 teaspoon fine granulated sugar
    sufficient ice

Use 10-ounce Collins glass and fill with soda. Stir and decorate with slice of lemon, cherry, and sprig of mint.

Old-Fashioned Cocktail

Shake 2 or 3 dashes of Angostura, then a splash of seltzer, on a lump of sugar. Muddle, add 2 cubes of ice, a twist of lemon peel, and a cherry, if desired. Pour in 1½ ounces of your favorite liquor, stir well and serve. (Simple syrup in place of lump sugar eliminates muddling and makes a much smoother drink; and if simple syrup is used, you don't need the seltzer.

Planter's Punch

    5 dashes Angostura Bitters
    1 oz. fresh lime juice
    1 oz. simple syrup or 2 teaspoons fine granulated sugar
    3 oz. heavy-bodied rum, such as Jamaica or Gold Label
    sufficient shaved ice

Place ingredients in mixing glass and shake vigorously. Pour unstrained into a 10-ounce Collins glass, fill with chilled carbonated water, stir slightly. Garnish with a slice of lemon and dust with nutmeg. Serve with straws. (Simple syrup instead of sugar makes a smoother drink.)

Rum Swizzle

    6 dashes Angostura Bitters
    1½ oz. light rum
    1 teaspoon fine granulated sugar
    juice of 1 fresh lime

Pour ingredients into a glass pitcher, add plenty of shaved ice, churn with swizzle stick until a fine, frothy head appears. Strain into cocktail glass and serve.

Singapore Sling

    3 dashes Angostura Bitters
    1 teaspoon fine granulated sugar
    ½ oz. lemon juice
    ¾ oz. cherry brandy
    1 oz. dry gin

Put into 10-ounce highball glass with 2 cubes crystal-clear ice. Fill with carbonated water, stir slightly. Twist lemon peel over top for oil, then drop into drink. Serve with a stir rod.

Toddy (cold)

    Place the rind of ½ lemon in an old-fashioned glass with 1 teaspoon granulated sugar and muddle thoroughly. Add a little carbonated water. Then place 1 cube of ice in the glass and pour 1 ounce of whiskey over it. Stir with stir rod and serve. (If a longer drink is desired, use a highball glass, 3 cubes of ice, and fill with carbonated water.)

Whiskey Sour

    3 generous dashes Angostura Bitters
    1½ oz. rye or bourbon whiskey
    ¾ oz. lemon juice
    1 teaspoon fine granulated sugar

Frappe and strain into Delmonico glass prepared with a slice of orange and a cherry.

Zombie (original and authentic Carioca recipe)

    1 oz. tropical heavy-bodied rum
    2 oz. Gold Label rum
    1 oz. White Label rum
    2 teaspoons apricot brandy
    ¾ oz. unsweetened pineapple juice
    ¾ oz. papaya juice
    1 teaspoon granulated sugar
    juice of 1 lime

Shake well with plenty of cracked ice and pour unstrained into a 12-ounce zombie glass. Float a splash of 151 proof tropical heavy-bodied rum on top. Spike on a toothpick in the order named: 1 green cherry, ½ inch pineapple stick, 1 red cherry. Decorate with this and a sprig of mint. Sprinkle powdered sugar over all and serve.

> Ah, my beloved, fill the cup that clears
> To-day of past regrets and future fears.
>
> Omar Khayyam

Drinks on the Mild Side

You will have some guests who do not care for alcoholic beverages and this, of course, includes the kiddies. The following are a few non-alcoholic drinks that have met with great approval at barbecues and outdoor parties. We hope they prove as successful at your own parties.

Campfire Coffee

old-fashioned coffee pot
4½ cups cold water
5 cups coarsely ground coffee
a few eggshells
¼ cup cold water
⅛ teaspoon salt

Bring water to a rolling boil. Remove from fire and add coffee and eggshells. Replace on grill and simmer slowly for 8 minutes (do not boil). Add ¼ cup cold water and salt to settle the grounds. Serve as soon as clear.

Clam-Juice Cocktail

1 quart very strong clam broth or juice which can be bought in market
1 demi-tasse catsup
2 dashes Tabasco sauce
½ teaspoon celery salt
1 teaspoon sugar dissolved in juice 2 lemons

Mix thoroughly and strain. Shake with ice. Put celery salt on top and serve.

Egg Phosphate

Use large glass half full of ice. Add one teaspoon of sugar, one teaspoon of acid phosphate, one whole egg. Shake well. Strain. Fill glass with carbonated water.

Florida Punch

1 can (6 oz.) frozen orange or tangerine juice
1 can (6 oz.) frozen grapefruit juice
1 #2 can pineapple juice
1 lemon or lime
3 cups water

Squeeze lemon or lime and combine with grapefruit juice in a large pitcher. Add the frozen juices and stir until melted. Pour over ice in tall glasses, or for a crowd, double the recipe and serve from a punch bowl.

Fog Horn

Into a large glass put a cube of ice, juice of half a lemon. Fill with ginger ale.

Grape-Juice Highball

Place the grape juice in an 8- or 10-ounce glass. Add a lump or two of ice and fill with carbonated water. Sugar may be added.

Grenadine Cooler

Use a large 12-ounce glass with 3 large cubes of ice, the juice of one lime, and one ounce of Grenadine syrup. Fill glass with chilled carbonated water, stir well.

Horse's Neck

Peel a whole lemon in one long string and place peel in a large glass so that one end hangs over the edge. Add two cubes of ice. Fill with ginger ale.

2. *Meats*

NOTHING satisfies the inner man so much as meat. Properly barbecued and marinated in its own rich, succulent juices, herbs, and perhaps a drop o' wine . . . ah, that is something for the very soul! Many a worthy artist of the pit or grill owes his well-deserved fame to knowledge of outdoor meat cookery.

BEEF

Charcoal-Broiled Steak

      1 4-pound steak 2½ inches thick
      salt and pepper
      butter

Beforehand Preparations: Trim away most excess fat so that drippings won't blaze too much. Gash the fat edges of the steak to prevent curling.

At the Grill: Build your charcoal fire and let it burn for about 45 minutes. At this point you should have a lively bed of coals covered with gray film but no active fire. Rub the grill or broiling rack well with the fat trimmings. This prevents meat from sticking and wafts a delicious appetite-whetting aroma into the air. Place the steak 6 or 7 inches from the hot coals. Grill first side to a dark crusty brown, for medium rareness about 12 minutes. Flip with fork and turner. Do not poke fork into lean meat, or you'll drip precious juices into the fire bed. If drippings flare up, water the flames down a little. Now salt and pepper the browned side. Brown the other side—again about 12 minutes. Season second side. Add a generous hunk of butter, and steak's on! Serves 4.

    TRAY BOY: *steak, fat trimmings, salt and pepper, butter*

Menu

      charcoal-broiled steak
      baked potatoes
      tossed green salad
      fruit and cheese
      cola, beer, or coffee

Variations on Charcoal-Broiled Steak

1. steak
2 cloves garlic
1 cup oil

Put garlic to soak in oil the night before your barbecue. Discard the garlic cloves. Pour the oil into shallow pan and place the steak in the oil for 5 minutes on each side. Grill.

2. One school of chefs prefers to marinate steak in oil overnight, adding juice of a lemon or ¼ cup of good wine vinegar to the marinade.

3. Soya sauce is a marvelous browning agent for all meat. Place 1 cup soya sauce in a glass or enamel dish (not aluminum) and marinate overnight.

4. *Planked Steak:* Place the finished steak on a preheated plank and surround with hashed brown potatoes, zucchini, stuffed peppers, broiled mushroom caps, succotash, glazed onions, asparagus tips, slices of tomato, or what have you. The trick here is to serve everything hot and gorgeous.

5. *Steak Sandwiches:* Prepare the steak and have ready warm French bread or frankfurter rolls and a bowl of butter with several brushes. Just before serving, let each person brush the butter on the warm bread and line up for cuts of steak. Serve with a large tray of crisp, chilled sliced carrots, Bermuda onions, tomatoes, pickles and relishes. Have ready dishes of spicy mustard and homemade chili sauce. Pile a bowl high with fresh potato chips, and you really have a meal.

Pan-Broiled Steak

a 4-pound steak, 1 inch thick
steak fat
salt and pepper

Beforehand Preparation: Remove all fat around the edges of steak.

At the Grill: Use a large cast-iron or steel skillet or a flat griddle. Rub well with beef-fat trimmings. Get the utensil smoking hot. Quickly sear the steak on both sides. Move to a cooler cooking surface, season, and broil until done as you desire. Pour off any excess fat that accumulates, since it will prevent frying the meat. This is a faster method than charcoal-broiling, so watch it carefully. This is an excellent way to do thinner cuts of beefsteak; the timing depends on the thickness. Thin minute steaks take about 1 minute on each side. Thicker steaks have to be turned several times to avoid sticking, and may require up to ten minutes. Serves 4.

TRAY BOY: *steak, fat, pepper mill, salt*

Menu

pan-broiled steak
scalloped-potato-and-onion casserole
Chinese cabbage and apple salad
hot rolls
greengage plums and cookies
iced coffee

Variations of Pan-Broiled Steak

1. Pan-broiled steak which has been marinated 15 minutes in a little brandy is fit for the gods.

2. For a fine wine sauce remove steak when done and add a tablespoon of butter, a mashed clove of garlic, and ½ cup of red wine. Let it boil up, stirring and scraping the pan for a few minutes while someone else is serving the steak. Pour into a bowl. Sprinkle with 2 tablespoons of chopped parsley and pass to the guests.

Salt-Broiled Steak

a steak, boneless, 2 to 3 inches ½ pound margarine
  thick 1 box of coarse salt
¼ pound butter

Beforehand Preparation: Take the steak out of the refrigerator about 2 hours before cooking. Melt the butter and margarine.

At the Grill: When your bed of charcoal is giving off a good, even, hot heat, prepare the steak in the following manner. Mix a bowl of salt and water until it has the consistency of a gooey mud pie. Spread ½ inch coating over the meat, then brown paper, cut to fit, which has been greased on both sides. Place in hand grill and close; turn raw side of steak up and repeat. Allow 10 to 15 minutes grilling time for each side. The salt will harden, sealing in the steak juice. Your steak will be crisp and dark brown when you knock off the salt. Cut into slices, dip in the butter sauce, and serve on slices of French bread. Or you may substitute your favorite barbecue sauce for butter. Serves 6–8.

TRAY BOY: *steak, salt, greased paper, butter or margarine*

Menu

steak
French bread
chef's salad *
strawberry-melon bowl
iced tea

* Menu items marked with an asterisk can be found elsewhere in the book by consulting the index.

Filet Mignon with Olive Sauce

6 filets mignon, 1 inch thick
3 tablespoons butter or
  margarine
2 tablespoons flour
1 beef cube dissolved in 1 cup
  hot water

2 tablespoons minced onion
3 tablespoons chopped olive
¼ cup chopped green pepper
½ cup sliced mushrooms
2 ripe tomatoes
oil

Beforehand Preparation: Prepare chopped vegetables, peel tomato, and slice mushrooms.

At the Grill: Melt butter or margarine in a skillet. Sauté onions and green pepper until soft. Remove vegetables and set aside. Add flour to juice in pan. Cook until flour begins to brown. Stir in beef-cube water and cook 3 minutes. Add all vegetables and olives. Cook 5 minutes. Brush filets with oil. Place in hand grill and broil quickly near the coals. They will not take long, so watch them carefully. Place on heated serving platter and cover with sauce. Serves 6.

TRAY BOY: *filets mignon, chopped vegetables, tomatoes, butter, flour, salt, pepper mill, oil, beef-cube water*

Menu

deviled eggs *
olives and celery
filet mignon with olive sauce
parsley potatoes
asparagus on toast
tossed salad
fruit, cheese, crackers
beer or ale

Braised Steak

3 pounds top-round steak,
   1 inch thick
¼ cup flour
2 tablespoons fat
1 chopped onion

1 teaspoon salt
¼ teaspoon pepper
1 teaspoon Worcestershire
   sauce
boiling water

Beforehand Preparation: Pound the flour into steak with a mallet.

At the Grill: Heat fat until sizzling hot in a heavy skillet. Add meat and brown on one side. Add chopped onion. Turn meat and brown on the other side. Season with salt, pepper, and Worcestershire sauce. Add boiling water to cover the bottom of the pan, cover, and simmer until steak is tender. Serves 4.

TRAY BOY: *steak, fat, onion, salt and pepper, Worcestershire sauce*

Menu

braised steak
potato casserole
tomatoes filled with cottage cheese
hot biscuits
pecan pie
coffee

Individual Barbecued Steaks

8 cubed steaks
8 rolls
butter
pepper

Sauce:
½ teaspoon garlic salt
3 tablespoons Worcester-
    shire sauce
2 tablespoons oil
6 tablespoons catsup
½ tablespoon salt
4 tablespoons red wine vinegar

Beforehand Preparation: Combine all the sauce ingredients and bring to a boil. Remove from the fire at once, cool for 5 minutes, and pour over the steaks. Marinate for 15 minutes.

At the Grill: Place the steaks in a hand grill and broil for 3 minutes on each side, basting once. Have the rolls toasting. Butter the rolls. Pop the steaks into the rolls. Dab with barbecue sauce, sprinkle with pepper and salt. Serves 8.

TRAY BOY: *steaks, sauce, rolls, butter, pepper mill, salt*

Menu

individual barbecued steaks
chef's salad *
homemade blueberry pie
coffee

Tenderized Round Steaks (Hawaiian Special)
Originated by our good friend, James T. Brown

First marinate for 24 hours:
a tender round steak, 3 pounds

Sauce:
2 cloves garlic
2 tablespoons green ginger
sprinkle of salt
1 cup sho-yu (soya sauce)
2 tablespoons sugar
½ cup saki, gin, rum, or
　whiskey

Mash! Do not chop the garlic and ginger; the flavor will be better. Add salt, sho-yu, sugar, ginger, and liquor. Mix thoroughly and marinate your meat in this for 24 hours, turning the meat now and then. If there is more meat than marinade, make some more. Put on your barbecue and cook rare, medium, or well done. Any vegetable will go well with this, and, of course, a "scuttle of suds." Serves 4.

TRAY BOY: *steak, basting sauce*

Menu

tenderized round steak
baked potatoes *
pick-and-choose salad *
pineapple turnovers
beer

Beefsteak à La Suisse

a round steak
½ cup flour
1 teaspoon salt
¼ teaspoon pepper
½ teaspoon paprika

Tomato Mixture:
1 cup coarsely-chopped onions
2 tablespoons bacon fat
1 #2 can tomatoes
½ cup chopped green pepper
1 bay leaf
2 cloves
1 tablespoon tomato paste
½ teaspoon salt
¼ teaspoon pepper
6 slices bacon

Beforehand Preparation: Order a boneless two-pound steak for four people. Cut about 1 inch thick. Mix the flour with salt, pepper, and paprika. Pound flour into meat with a tenderizer mallet. Pound hard. Sauté the onions in fat until transparent. Combine tomatoes, green pepper, bay leaf, cloves, tomato paste, salt and pepper.

At the Grill: Fry bacon until crisp in a cast-iron skillet. Remove the bacon, save. Quickly sauté the steak in hot fat until brown on both sides. Add tomato mixture. Cover and simmer about 45 minutes until very tender. Carve and place on hot plates. Sprinkle with finely chopped bacon. Serve with potatoes which have been baked in the coals while steak was cooking. For 4.

TRAY BOY: *bacon, steak, tomato mixture, baking potatoes*

Menu

beeksteak à la suisse
baked potatoes *
poppyseed rolls
pineapple-and-cottage-cheese salad
iced tea or coffee

Delmonico Roast

a 4-rib rolled sirloin roast
2 cups A-1 sauce * or Mexican barbecue sauce *

Beforehand Preparation: Have the beef rolled with a nice thick jacket of suet on the outside. Remove from the refrigerator several hours before cooking time.

At the Grill: Secure the meat on a spit over medium-low heat and turn about every 5 minutes, basting with the sauce. Plan your cooking time to be 17 minutes per dressed pound if very rare and 30 minutes per pound if it is to be well done—average time about 23 minutes per pound. Arrange a drip pan below to catch the juices. Remove from the spit and serve hot with skimmed, unthickened drip-pan gravy. Serves 10.

TRAY BOY: *roast, sauce*

Menu

olives, salted nuts
Delmonico roast
roasted potatoes *
mixed green salad
strawberry whip on sponge cake *
coffee or beer

SERVICE NOTE: *Rolled roast or rolled top round can be roasted as above.*

Outdoor Salisbury Steak

3 pounds hamburger
2 eggs
2 tablespoons melted butter
2 tablespoons red wine
1 tablespoon onion juice

1 teaspoon salt
½ teaspoon freshly ground
   pepper
2 tablespoons fat
2 tablespoons wine

Beforehand Preparation: Have your butcher remove all fat from lean top round. Put through grinder once. Beat eggs until lemony. Lightly mix all ingredients, except wine and fat. Form into one large cake 1½ inches thick.

At the Grill: Grill on a cast-iron skillet or in a wire hand grill. We prefer the cast-iron skillet because none of the juices are lost. Heat skillet, add fat, and sear the cake. Flip with 2 broad spatulas. As soon as the second side is brown, remove skillet to a cooler section of grill and continue cooking about 6 to 7 minutes. Test for doneness. Add a bit of wine to pan juice and make a thin gravy. Serve piping hot. Cut into long, thin slices and place between hot buttered frankfurter rolls, or cut into pie-shaped wedges and serve on toasted buttered English-muffin halves. Add gravy. Serves 6 to 8.

TRAY BOY: *meat cake, fat, rolls or muffins, wine*

Menu

salisbury steak
rolls or muffins
hashed-brown potatoes *
Southern fruit salad *
red wine or beer

Tournedos

2 pounds filet mignon
salt
pepper

chopped chives
butter or margarine
barbecue sauce

Beforehand Preparation: Have filet mignon cut into 1-inch-thick rounds.

At the Grill: Salt and pepper the meat and sprinkle with chives. Dip in your favorite barbecue sauce. Sauté quickly on buttered flat griddle. Serve on rounds of bread which have been sautéed in butter at the same time. Pour on more barbecue sauce. Serves 4.

TRAY BOY: *filet-mignon rounds, salt, pepper mill, chives, butter or margarine, barbecue sauce*

Menu

tournedos
tossed garden salad
cherry pie
choice of beverage
beer or coffee

Beef Roll-Ups

8 cubed steaks
8 slices boiled ham
mustard
flour
salt

pepper
2 tablespoons fat
1 can beef bouillon
¼ cup red wine
1 small can mushroom caps

Beforehand Preparation: Flatten the steaks and spread with mustard. Place on each a slice of ham about the same size as the steak. Roll into "cigars" and tie at both ends to preserve shapes. Dredge with flour mixed with salt and pepper.

At the Grill: Brown the beef rolls in hot fat. Add the beef bouillon and wine and simmer, covered, 20 minutes. Add the mushrooms and their juice if more liquid is desired. Cover and cook slowly for 6 minutes longer. Thicken the gravy with a little flour. Serves 4.

TRAY BOY: *beef roll-ups, fat, bouillon, wine, mushrooms, flour*

Menu

avocado-pear dunking sauce and crackers *
beef roll-ups
fluffy rice *
broccoli vinaigrette
baked pear
coffee or red wine

Barbecued Beef Short Ribs

3 pounds lean short ribs
1 cup tomato juice
1 teaspoon salt
½ teaspoon fresh pepper
2 cloves mashed garlic

¼ teaspoon powdered cloves
1 teaspoon brown sugar
1 teaspoon dry mustard
½ cup red wine vinegar
⅛ teaspoon thyme

Beforehand Preparation: Make a marinade of all the above ingredients, except for the meat. Beat until well-mixed. Place the meat in a glass bowl. Pour the marinade over and allow to stand 10 hours in the refrigerator. Remove about 2 hours before using.

At the Grill: Grill meat over coals which are hot, but not burning, for about 25 minutes. Turn and baste frequently. Serves 6.

TRAY BOY: *marinated short ribs, marinade*

Menu

cheese tray and crackers *
beef short ribs
baked potatoes *
grilled tomatoes *
fresh fruit
lemonade

Western-Style Pot Roast

6 pounds rolled bottom round
3 tablespoons fat
2 tablespoons flour
1 teaspoon salt
½ teaspoon pepper

1 cup sour cream
1 cup sherry wine
8 small carrots
8 small onions
4 stalks celery, cut in half-inch
    lengths

Beforehand Preparation: Dredge the roast with a mixture of flour, salt, and freshly ground pepper.

At the Grill: Heat the fat in a Dutch oven until a drop of water bounces in it. Sear the meat all over. Add the sherry wine and sour cream. Cover and simmer for 1½ hours. Turn the roast and toss vegetables on top of meat. Cook for another hour. Serve with gravy in the pan. Serves 8.

TRAY BOY: *dredged roast, fat, sour cream, sherry, carrots, onions, celery*

Menu

avocado dunking sauce and potato chips *
western-style pot roast
stuffed baked potatoes
hearts of lettuce salad
fruit and cookies
coffee or sherry

Andalusian Pot Roast

3 to 4 pounds beef round
1 cup grape juice

Marinade:
2 tablespoons olive oil
2 tablespoons finely chopped
    onion
4 tablespoons lemon juice
5 peppercorns
½ bay leaf
1 small clove mashed garlic
3 tablespoons coarsely chopped
    parsley
2 or 3 tarragon leaves, or ¼
    teaspoon dried tarragon

Beforehand Preparation: Have your butcher give you a solid piece of beef with very little fat. Bring the marinade to a boil; lower flame and simmer slowly for 5 minutes. Put the meat in a crock and pour over the marinade. Cover for 24 hours, turning several times.

At the Grill: Put meat and marinade in a Dutch oven, add grape juice, cover closely and cook 2 or 3 hours, turning occasionally, adding a very little water to keep from sticking.

TRAY BOY: *beef in marinade, grape juice*

Menu

antipasti *
pot roast
roasted potatoes *
string beans
popovers and crabapple jelly
fruits steeped in rum
coffee

Ranger Stew

1½ pounds lean beef cut into 2-inch cubes
1 mashed clove garlic
1 bay leaf
5 whole peppers
1 teaspoon chili powder
1 tablespoon Worcestershire sauce
½ cup vinegar
½ cup water
3 tablespoons catsup
2 chopped onions

Beforehand Preparation: Place meat in large bowl, add all other ingredients, except onion, and marinate 3 or 4 hours.

At the Grill: Put meat in Dutch oven or other heavy kettle, add onions and marinade, cover closely, and let simmer 2 hours or until meat is tender. Add a little additional water if needed. Serves 6.

TRAY BOY: *beef in marinade, onion*

Menu

pickled oysters
wilted cucumbers
ranger stew
grilled tomatoes *
peach cobbler with lemon sauce
beer or ale

Swedish Meat Balls

½ pound chuck beef
¼ pound veal
¼ pound pork
½ cup fine dried bread crumbs
1 cup milk
2 tablespoons minced onion
4 tablespoons fat

1 egg, slightly beaten
1 teaspoon salt
¼ teaspoon pepper
a pinch of allspice
3 tablespoons flour
1 cup beef bouillon

Beforehand Preparation: Have the butcher put the meat through the grinder twice. Soak the crumbs in milk. Combine meat, crumbs, and milk; mix well. Sauté the onions in the fat until soft. Reserve fat. Add the onions, egg, salt, pepper, and allspice to the meat. Form into very tiny balls. Roll in flour.

At the Grill: Brown the meat balls on all sides in hot fat in a heavy skillet. Remove meat balls. Blend flour with fat remaining in the skillet. Add the bouillon and cook until smooth. Return the meat balls to the pan and simmer slowly for 20 minutes. Serve very hot. Serves 6.

TRAY BOY: *meat balls, fat, beef bouillon*

Menu

smorgasbord *
Swedish meat balls
kidney beans seasoned with vinegar and brown sugar
pumpernickel bread
figs with cream cheese
beer or coffee

Beef Tartare

This is for men with grizzly-bear hair on their chests:

2 pounds of top-grade ground lean beef	1 tablespoon minced chives
1 clove mashed garlic	1 tablespoon minced parsley
	2 Bermuda onions

Beforehand Preparation: Sprinkle garlic (mashed in garlic press), chives, and parsley over the meat. Mix lightly and form into 4-inch patties. Slice onions and separate into rings.

At the Grill: Heat a greased griddle until very hot. Sear patties for 15 seconds on each side. Place on toasted rolls, top with raw onion rings and serve with your choice of chili sauce, 1, 2, or 3.* For 6.

TRAY BOY: *beef patties, chili sauce, rolls, onion rings*

Menu

beef tartare or rolls with onion rings
chili sauce *
dill pickles
deviled eggs *
tossed salad with piquante dressing *
brandied peaches
cuba libre or coffee

Beef Cakes in Red Wine

1¼ pounds lean beef
2 cups red wine
½ teaspoon garlic juice

3 tablespoons butter
freshly ground pepper
salt

Beforehand Preparation: Shape meat into 4 cakes. Pour wine and garlic juice over them and marinate at room temperature for several hours. Save the wine. Drain and dry the cakes on paper toweling.

At the Grill: Heat the butter in a skillet. Brown cakes quickly, turn and season. Brown other side. Pour over cakes enough wine to make a sauce when blended with butter and juices in the pan. Simmer for a few minutes and serve on crisp toast with wine sauce. Serves 4.

TRAY BOY: *beef cakes, butter, salt, pepper mill, wine marinade*

Menu

beef cakes with burgundy sauce on toast
asparagus tips with hollandaise sauce
peach shortcake
red wine

Beef Cakes in Barbecue Sauce

3 pounds ground beef
1 teaspoon hickory-smoked salt
1/4 teaspoon pepper
4 English muffins

Sauce:
1 clove mashed garlic
2 tablespoons oil
1 chopped onion
1 cup tomato juice
1 teaspoon dry mustard
1 tablespoon A-1 sauce
2 tablespoons dry white wine
salt and pepper to taste

Beforehand Preparation: Mix beef, salt and pepper. Form into 4-inch patties, 3/4 inch thick.

At the Grill: Grill beef cakes quickly until brown on both sides. Set aside. Heat a large skillet, add oil, garlic, and chopped onion. Cook until golden brown. Add remaining ingredients. Simmer for 10 minutes. Add beef cakes. Simmer for 5 minutes, turning once. Serve on split toasted English muffins with plenty of sauce. Serves 8.

TRAY BOY: *beef cakes, oil, garlic, onion, tomato juice, mustard, A-1 sauce, wine, salt, pepper, English muffins*

Menu

beef cakes in barbecue sauce on muffins
hashed brown potatoes *
tossed green salad with sour cream dressing *
canteloupe filled with ice cream
ale or coffee

Barbecued Meat Loaf

1¾ pounds ground beef
¼ pound ground pork
1 cup soft bread crumbs
1 cup tomato juice
1 egg, slightly beaten
¼ cup minced onion

2 tablespoons minced parsley
½ teaspoon thyme
2 teaspoons salt
¼ teaspoon pepper
½ cup Tabasco barbecue
    sauce *

Beforehand Preparation: Mix meat with bread crumbs, tomato juice, and slightly beaten egg. With a fork lightly stir in onion, parsley, thyme, salt, and pepper. Shape into a high, rounded cake.

At the Grill: Pour 2 cups of water into Dutch oven. Place meat loaf over grill in a Dutch oven and cook covered for about an hour or more. Baste with sauce from time to time. Serves 6.

TRAY BOY: *meat loaf, barbecue sauce, water*

Menu

barbecued meat loaf
roasted potatoes *
co'n pone *
grapes
coffee

Quick Stew

2 cups cooked beef or other
    meat, sliced
2 cups cooked vegetables
3 tablespoons chopped parsley
salt

pepper
1 8-oz. can tomato soup
1 cup leftover gravy
½ cup beer

Beforehand Preparation: Dice meat and combine with vegetables.

At the Grill: Pour tomato soup, gravy, and beer into a skillet. Stir in meat, vegetables, and parsley. Season to taste. Simmer 20 minutes, or until mixture is heated through and sauce is thoroughly mixed. Serve in large bowls. Serves 4.

TRAY BOY: *tomato soup, gravy, beer, meat, vegetables, parsley, salt, pepper mill*

Menu

quick stew
rye-bread toast
ice-cream roll
iced coffee

Cuban-Style Chopped Beef and Rice

2 tablespoons bacon fat
1 pound of coarsely ground
    flank beef
1 small green pepper
1 small onion
3½ cups tomatoes

1 cup uncooked rice
1 tablespoon salt
½ teaspoon pepper
½ teaspoon of cumin
pinch of saffron

Beforehand Preparation: Chop the pepper and onion.

At the Grill: Heat the fat in a heavy pot with lid. Add the beef, green pepper, and onion. Stir until meat is separated and browned. Add tomatoes, rice, and seasonings. Cover and cook 25 minutes, or until rice is tender. Serves 4.

TRAY BOY: *fat, meat, salt, pepper mill, cumin, saffron, green pepper, onion, tomatoes, rice*

Menu

Cuban-style chopped beef and rice
cabbage and onion slaw
French bread
preserved guava halves and cream cheese
Cuban-style coffee

Spaghetti and Some Wonderful Sauces

¾ pound ground round steak †
1 small can tomato paste
1 #2 can strained tomatoes
½ cup olive oil
2 medium sized minced onions
½ teaspoon orégano
1 clove mashed garlic
1 teaspoon salt

dash of Tabasco sauce
1 cup red wine
½ cup minced parsley
¼ pound grated Parmesan
  cheese
2 packages thin spaghetti
¼ cup butter
salt

Beforehand Preparation: Cook tomato paste and tomatoes together for 30 minutes. Strain. Prepare vegetables.

At the Grill: Heat the oil in a large, heavy pan. Sauté onions until transparent. Add the tomatoes, orégano, garlic, salt, and Tabasco. Cover and simmer 10 minutes. Add wine and meat. Simmer for 20 minutes. Meanwhile on another part of the grill heat a large pot of water. Bring to a fierce boil. Add 2 teaspoons salt and spaghetti. Boil briskly for 15 minutes or until tender. Drain and add butter; mix thoroughly. Place in a large bowl. Keep hot. Now add the cooked sauce, parsley, and half the cheese. Toss and mix well as if it were a salad. Serve at once with the remaining cheese in a dish. Serves 8 to 10.

TRAY BOY: *oil, onions, tomato mixture, orégano, garlic, salt, Tabasco sauce, wine, ground meat, spaghetti, butter, parsley, grated cheese*

Menu

tossed green salad
spaghetti with meat sauce
garlic bread *
fruit and cheese
beer, ale, or red wine

2 tins of *anchovies* and a bottle of capers may be substituted for the meat.

† Make *meat balls* exactly as for Swedish meat balls. Brown in oil and add the sauce ingredients (eliminating the ground beef) in the order given above. Pour over hot spaghetti and serve.

Barbecue Brunch

2 cans corned-beef hash
1 teaspoon onion juice
1 teaspoon Worcestershire
   sauce

3 tablespoons bacon fat
4 eggs
paprika

Beforehand Preparation: Mix the hash with onion juice and Worcestershire sauce.

At the Grill: Heat a flat griddle. Grease with bacon fat. Spread corned-beef-hash mixture on griddle and form into a round cake ¾ inch thick. Brown one side and flip whole cake in one piece with spatula. Brown second side. Cut in pie-shaped wedges and place on heated plates. Make indentations to accommodate eggs. While hash is cooking, bring 1 inch water to a simmer in a shallow skillet. Carefully drop in eggs. Poach until firm. Remove from water with slotted spoon or spatula. Place on corned-beef hash. Sprinkle with paprika. Serve with catsup if desired. Serves 4.

TRAY BOY: *bacon fat, corned-beef-hash mixture, eggs, paprika*

Menu

pineapple juice
corned-beef hash with poached eggs
toasted English muffins and marmalade
coffee

Corned Beef and Kidney Beans

1 can kidney beans
1 cup cooked tomatoes
½ cup red wine
1 12-ounce can corned beef
2 medium onions

2 tablespoons butter or
  margarine
1 tablespoon brown sugar
dash of Tabasco sauce

Beforehand Preparation: Slice onions thin, separate into rings. Cube corned beef.

At the Grill: Sauté onions in butter until golden brown. Combine with beans, tomatoes and wine. Add sugar, corned beef, and Tabasco sauce. Cover and simmer for a half an hour. Serves 6.

> TRAY BOY: *kidney beans, tomatoes, red wine, corned beef, onions, butter or margarine, brown sugar, Tabasco sauce*

Menu

corned beef and kidney beans
split toasted rolls
green salad with Roquefort dressing *
lemon sherbet and little cakes
coffee

Better-Than-Ever Meat

6 or more slices leftover roast
    beef or lamb
2 tablespoons bacon fat or lard
1 small onion
1 clove garlic
1 teaspoon salt

¼ teaspoon freshly ground
    pepper
2 tablespoons Worcestershire
    sauce
1 tablespoon vinegar
4 tablespoons chili sauce

Beforehand Preparation: Slice leftover meat and trim away excess fat. Chop onion and garlic.

At the Grill: Melt bacon fat or lard in skillet, add onion and garlic, and cook slowly until tender. Add slices of meat and mixture of other ingredients, cover skillet tightly, and cook about 15 minutes, adding a very little water if necessary and basting meat with sauce occasionally. Serves 4.

TRAY BOY: *sliced meat, chopped onion and garlic, Worcestershire sauce, vinegar, chili sauce, fat, salt, pepper mill*

Menu

tomato juice
barbecued leftover roast
carrot balls
baked potatoes
endive salad
fruit sherbet
coffee

SERVICE NOTE: *This may be cooked in a casserole in the oven, and is an excellent way to use leftover meat.*

Chili Con Carne

Another recipe from our friend in Hawaii, James T. Brown

Get 2¼ lbs. of round steak and cut the meat into small pieces. Put to one side with a chunk of suet and a good bone with some marrow in it.

Now, do not throw up your hands in horror, for we are the Masters and not the following:

Four to five onions chopped, 10 to 15 buds of garlic, either chopped or run through the presser. Lay these to one side. One teaspoon of cumin seed. This must be ground, for no maker of chili con carne in his right mind would put in cumin until it had been ground. Take that out of the mortar and toss in one tablespoon orégano, two laurel leaves, and two minced bell peppers with the seeds. Yes, the seeds, but not the white pulp. Now a pinch of fine herbs. There must be a large can of tomatoes, and the frijoles or Mexican red beans. Never, never use kidney beans. Take about 3 cups of the frijoles and let soak in water overnight. Drain the water off.

Now you'll need a pot about 9 inches wide and 8 inches tall. Nothing smaller than that. Put the beans in the pot and pour in the canned tomatoes along with the onions and the garlic. Let them get warmed up a bit; then in goes the meat, chopped in small pieces. Please never use ground hamburger! Add the bone and the suet. When that gets heated up, in goes the cumin, orégano, a good tablespoon of paprika, the laurel leaves, the minced bell peppers with the seeds, and the pinch of fine herbs. With the wooden spoon stir up the ingredients that they will be properly wedded. When that ceremony has been completed, have some chili powder ready alongside. Here is where your conscience must be your guide. Stir in at least two good tablespoonfuls of the chili powder. Now one tablespoon salt, with just enough water to keep the mixture in an ebullient state. Go away for a while, and in about 20 minutes come back and taste to see how the chili flavor is taking hold. I would add another tablespoon of chili powder, but perchance your guests would think it too hot.

You fix that to suit yourself. Now that you have that going, sit down in your easy chair with a highball near. If you stir once in a while it will not hurt, but if you don't it will take care of itself. If the gravy is not quite red enough, toss in a can or two of tomato sauce. But keep plenty of water in the pot so that it will not get dry. When the meat and frijoles are tender, cover it up and put away in the refrigerator for 4 days, so that all the ingredients will get thoroughly aware of each other's presence. Then gather the guests around, give them something to drink, heat, and ladle the steaming hot chili con carne out to them in soup plates. Beer, claret wine, or cabernet goes well with it. If you have some good spaghetti cheese, some of this sprinkled on top will give a good taste. If you wish to go extra fine, put in some minced olives during the last part of the cooking.

I have made it hundreds of times and never had a cross word yet. Your guests will acclaim you the best of all, and never know that there are onions and garlic in it. On my word!

LAMB

California's No. 1 Son

Mouton en Mer Rouge

1 leg of lamb, boned
3 slices fat bacon
2 tablespoons butter
2 tablespoons flour

1 cup Madeira wine
1 tablespoon currant jelly
salt and pepper to taste
dash of red pepper

Beforehand Preparation: Trim meat for roasting and wipe with dry cloth. Chop the bacon.

At the Grill: Put the bacon in a skillet and fry until crisp. Remove bacon. Put the spit through the lamb and brush with bacon grease. Add 1 cup of water to remaining bacon grease. Turn the lamb often, basting with the skillet broth. When the meat is properly roasted (approximately 2½ hours), place the butter in the skillet and blend in flour. Add wine, currant jelly, and seasonings to make a medium thick sauce. Serves 8.

TRAY BOY: *leg of lamb, bacon, butter, flour, Madeira wine, jelly, salt, pepper*

Menu

mouton en mer rouge
macaroni sprinkled with bacon crumbles
hot biscuits
Waldorf salad
rhubarb baked with honey
Madeira wine

Mock Venison

a small leg of lamb
2 tablespoons bacon drippings

Marinade:
1½ cups red wine vinegar
1½ cups water
4 slices onion
1 teaspoon orégano
2 teaspoons salt
1 tablespoon crushed juniper
   berries
¼ teaspoon pepper
4 whole peppercorns
1 teaspoon caraway seeds

Beforehand Preparation: Trim lamb carefully. Boil marinade gently 10 minutes. Pour over the lamb, adding more water if needed. Let stand 24 hours.

At the Grill: Heat the marinade and pour in bacon drippings. Stir until well mixed. Spit the lamb and turn often, basting with marinade. The lamb will take somewhere between 2 to 2½ hours. Test before removing from spit to see that there is no pink meat. Serves 6 to 8.

TRAY BOY: *drained leg of lamb, bacon drippings, marinade*

Menu

roast mock venison
grilled whole potatoes *
currant jelly, sweet pickles
shredded-carrot-and-lettuce salad
icebox cake
coffee

SERVICE NOTE: *If you want to cut down time of outdoor roasting, you can cook the lamb in covered roasting pan until half done, and then finish on your outdoor spit.*

Acadian Roast Mutton

1 leg of mutton
2 tablespoons butter
2 tablespoons flour

Marinade:
1 pint white wine
½ cup vinegar
½ pint olive oil
½ cup sliced onion
½ cup sliced carrot
1 tablespoon chopped parsley
1 tablespoon chopped shallot
1 clove garlic
½ teaspoon thyme
salt and pepper to taste

Beforehand Preparation: Have your butcher bone the mutton. Put mutton in large bowl. Simmer marinade gently ¾ hour. Pour over mutton, cool, cover, and keep in refrigerator 2 days, turning occasionally.

At the Grill: Remove the mutton from marinade. Place on spit and roast beside fire, basting occasionally with marinade. Reserve one cup of marinade. When mutton is done, approximately 2½ hours, blend butter and flour in saucepan, gradually add marinade, and stir over fire to make a smooth sauce.

TRAY BOY: *leg of mutton, marinade, flour, butter*

Menu

avocado canapés *
Acadian roast mutton
scalloped potatoes
chiffonade salad *
hot rolls
coffee

Chef's Mixed Grill

6 lamb or mutton chops
6 small slices calf's liver
6 oysters, shelled

6 strips bacon
barbecue sauce, California-
    style *

Beforehand Preparation: Trim chops. Remove outside skin and veins from liver. If liver seems to be tough, steam for five minutes just before using.

At the Grill: Place chops on well-greased wire broiler or on large grill over fire and broil quickly, first on one side and then on the other. Broil slowly until done, turning twice. Baste with sauce. Pan-fry liver, oysters, and bacon, tending carefully so that all will be done at the same time. Baste with sauce. Arrange on plates and serve at once, passing barbecue sauce. Serves 6.

TRAY BOY: *chops, liver, oysters, bacon, barbecue sauce*

Menu

tomato-and-cheese canapés
mixed grill with French-fried potatoes
green peas
celery salad
tropical compote with wine sauce *
red wine

Stuffed Lamb al Fresco

1 shoulder of lamb
1 clove garlic
pepper
salt
½ cup red wine
1 teaspoon lemon juice
2 thin slices of lemon peel
1 tablespoon onion juice
2 tablespoons chopped mint
½ teaspoon rosemary

Stuffing:
2 cups bread crumbs
2 tablespoons margarine
2 tablespoons chopped onion
2 tablespoons chopped celery
½ teaspoon poultry seasoning
salt and pepper
water

Beforehand Preparation: For this you'll need a boned shoulder of lamb. Rub the meat with a cut clove of garlic and sprinkle with salt and pepper. Mix the ingredients for the dressing. Season to taste with salt and pepper. Add enough water to moisten slightly. Fill the pocket and spread the dressing on the meat. Roll the meat and tie. Make a basting sauce by simmering the wine, lemon juice and peel, onion juice, mint, and rosemary for 15 minutes.

At the Grill: Stick the spit skewer through the center of the roll. Roast over lively coals for 1½ to 2 hours. Turn and baste frequently. Serves 6.

TRAY BOY: *lamb, barbecue sauce*

Menu

stuffed lamb al fresco
parsley boiled potatoes
sautéed mushrooms
Belgian endive salad
hot buttered rolls
sugared fresh pineapple sprinkled with Cointreau
demitasse

Chops à La Henry the Eighth

6 lamb or mutton chops   1 teaspoon of salt
1 clove of garlic   ¼ teaspoon of pepper

Beforehand Preparation: Have your butcher cut lamb chops 2½ inches thick. Rub them with a cut clove of garlic and season with salt and freshly ground pepper.

At the Grill: Place the chops directly on your grill about 7 inches above a bed of lively coals. Grill until brown. Turn and brown the other side. Allow about 15 minutes for each side depending on the thickness. While the chops are cooking prepare the hashed-brown potatoes. Place on piping hot plates. Serves 6.

TRAY BOY: *seasoned chops, diced potatoes*

Menu

lamb or mutton chops
mint sauce or jelly
zucchini
hashed-brown potatoes
melon-ball fruit cup
iced tea

Grilled Loin of Lamb

a loin of lamb, 4 to 5 pounds
1 clove of garlic
1 teaspoon of salt

pepper
1½ cups of A-1 barbecue
  sauce * with mint

Beforehand Preparation: A split loin of lamb should be divided into six thick portions cut only three-quarters of the way through the bone. Rub with cut clove of garlic, sprinkle with salt, and grind on fresh pepper.

At the Grill: Run the skewer from your spit directly through the center of the loin lengthwise. Secure closely. Attach to the spit. Turn often to insure even cooking and baste with sauce. The roast should be done in 45 minutes. Test for doneness. Complete the division of chops and serve on hot plates. Serves 6.

TRAY BOY: *loin of lamb, A-1 barbecue sauce*

Menu

loin of lamb
minted peas cooked with finely chopped onion
hot potato salad
celery, olives, and carrot sticks
cheese and crackers
iced coffee

Chickasaw Lamb Filets

2 pounds uncooked lamb cut
   in 1-inch strips
3 tablespoons chili sauce
butter

Marinade:
3 tablespoons olive oil
2 tablespoons vinegar
2 tablespoons chopped onion
2 tablespoons chopped parsley
salt and pepper to taste

Beforehand Preparation: Have the butcher cut the meat, preferably from a leg of lamb, pounding the strips to flatten. Mix marinade, put into a bowl and add the lamb fillets. Cover and let stand in refrigerator 10 or 12 hours.

At the Grill: Grease a large skillet with very little butter. When hot put in the lamb filets and sauté on both sides until brown and tender. When done take from skillet, add marinade and chili sauce. Blend well. Return the filets to the skillet. Heat well and serve at once.

TRAY BOY: *lamb filets in marinade, chili sauce, butter*

Menu

   melon with prosciutto *
   Chickasaw lamb filets
   new potatoes with parsley
   artichoke salad
   garlic bread *
   biscuit tortoni
   coffee

SERVICE NOTE: *Biscuit tortoni is easy to make at home. Make it the day before, keep in the freezing section of the refrigerator until needed.*

Irish Ale Stew

3 pounds lamb cut for stew
flour
salt and pepper
2 tablespoons fat
1½ cups ale
1 cup water

1 bay leaf
12 small onions
1 bunch small carrots
9 small potatoes
2 cups tender string beans

Beforehand Preparation: Mix flour, salt and pepper, and roll lamb pieces in it. Prepare vegetables. Cut carrots in strips.

At the Grill: Heat the fat in a Dutch oven or heavy pot with lid. Brown the meat all over. Add the ale, bay leaf, and 1 cup of boiling water. Cover and simmer for 1 hour. Add vegetables, boiling water to cover, and simmer for another hour. Season further, if necessary. Add flour mixed with cold water to thicken. Serves 6.

TRAY BOY: *lamb, fat, ale, water, bay leaf, onions, carrots, potatoes, string beans, flour, salt, pepper*

Menu

Irish ale stew
hot biscuits
apple pie with cheese
beer or ale

Lamb Rolls

1 pound lean lamb
½ teaspoon garlic juice
¼ cup chopped celery

freshly ground pepper
1 teaspoon salt
4 canned peach or pear halves

Beforehand Preparation: Have your butcher grind a pound of lean lamb shoulder. Chop celery very fine.

At the Grill: Mix meat, garlic juice, celery, salt, and freshly ground pepper to taste. Mix lightly until well-blended. Form into 8 rolls about 3 inches long. Grill the lamb rolls until they are browned on all sides (about 15 minutes). Grill peach or pear halves for eight minutes and serve with the lamb. Toast the frankfurter rolls. Serves 4.

TRAY BOY: *lamb, garlic juice, celery, pepper mill, salt, peach or pear halves*

Menu

raw-vegetable platter *
lamb rolls
grilled peaches or pears
toasted frankfurter rolls
avocado and seedless-grape salad *
red wine

Braised Kidneys

6 lamb kidneys
6 slices bread
butter
2 teaspoons dry mustard

1 teaspoon Worcestershire
   sauce
salt and pepper to taste

Beforehand Preparation: Split open the kidneys, let stand in boiling water a few minutes, drain, and run a metal skewer through each kidney to hold open and flat.

At the Grill: Butter the kidneys lightly on each side, place on a greased wire broiler, and broil first on one side and then on the other. Meanwhile cream 3 tablespoons of butter. Add mustard, Worcestershire sauce, and salt, and pepper to taste. Toast bread, butter lightly, place one kidney on each slice, and spread with seasoned butter. Serves 6.

> TRAY BOY: *kidneys, bread, butter, mustard, Worcestershire sauce, pepper mill, salt*

Menu

broiled cocktail sausages *
braised kidneys on toast
broiled tomatoes *
pickles, olives and celery
brandied peaches
little cakes
coffee

Real Indian Curry

2 tablespoons butter or oil
1 onion finely minced
chopped peel and juice of a
    lime
2 tablespoons grated fresh
    coconut
2 small pieces crystallized
    ginger

½ teaspoon ground cloves
1 tablespoon curry powder
2 cups bouillon
1 pound lean boneless lamb,
    veal or pork
salt

Beforehand Preparation: Prepare onion, coconut, ginger, and lime. Cut meat into 1-inch cubes.

At the Grill: Heat the butter in a skillet. Sauté onions and lime peel until onion begins to take on color. Add lime juice, coconut, cloves, ginger, and curry powder. Cook for 10 minutes over slow heat. Add bouillon and meat. Cover and simmer very slowly for an hour, adding water if necessary. Salt to taste. Serves 6.

TRAY BOY: *butter, lime peel and juice, onion, coconut, ginger, cloves, curry powder, bouillon, meat, salt*

Menu

chunks of fresh roasted coconut
real Indian curry
condiment tray: chutney, fresh shredded coconut, sliced
    tomatoes, chopped parsley, chopped nuts, raisins
fluffy saffron rice
tossed green salad *
ice cream
tea

Lamburgers and Bacon

a pound lamb cushion, ground | ¼ teaspoon pepper
1 egg | 12 strips bacon
1 teaspoon seasoned salt | A-1 barbecue sauce *

Mix the lamb, eggs, salt and pepper into rolls about 1½-inch thick and about 6 inches long. Skirt sides with bacon and secure with toothpicks. Dip lamburgers into barbecue sauce and place on grill. Brown all over, turning several times. Baste with sauce. Entire cooking time will be about 15 minutes. Serves 6.

Lamburgers and Twisters

Prepare lamburgers as above, minus the bacon skirts. Grill for five minutes. Remove from grill and wrap in a ribbon of biscuit dough (see Twisters). Impale on a skewer and finish cooking until dough is done (about 10 minutes).

SERVICE NOTE: *Lamburgers and lamb rolls are out of the ordinary and should be made from inexpensive cuts of meat. Serve them on toasted frankfurter rolls and have ready bowls of home-made chutney, watermelon pickles, sweet relish and a platter of sliced beefsteak tomatoes—a bowl of fruit and plate of cheese would provide a fitting and oh-so-easy dessert.*

VEAL

The Continental Chef's Delight

Pan-Broiled Veal Cutlets

a 2-pound veal cutlet, 1 inch
  thick
1 clove garlic
1 teaspoon salt

1 teaspoon marjoram
¼ teaspoon pepper
1 piece salt pork
2 tablespoons sherry (optional)

Beforehand Preparation: Have the butcher pound the cutlet a little when you buy it. Mix salt, pepper, and marjoram.

At the Grill: Rub the cutlet with a cut clove of garlic and season with the mixture. Try out the piece of salt pork in a skillet with a cover. Sear the veal on both sides. Add the sherry, which will tenderize the meat and add flavor. Cook slowly, covered, until very tender (about 45 minutes). Serve with any good barbecue sauce. Serves 4.

TRAY BOY: *cutlet, herb and spice mixture, garlic, salt pork, sherry*

Menu

antipasto *
veal cutlet
noodles
combination vegetable salad *
cheese cake
red wine or sherry

French Veal in a Dutch Oven

2 pounds veal steaks
1 quart boiling water
½ cup sliced onion
1 teaspoon salt
⅛ teaspoon fresh ground
    pepper

½ cup sauterne
¾ cup cream
3 tablespoons flour
1 tablespoon brown sugar
3 tablespoons butter

Beforehand Preparation: Cut veal into portions for serving.

At the Grill: Melt sugar in heavy kettle, then add onion and stir until coated. Add meat. Sear and pour in boiling water, returning latter to a boil. Cover closely and simmer until meat is almost tender. Next cream together salt, pepper, flour, and butter. Add to veal, stirring regularly until gravy is thick and smooth. Add wine and cream, cover and simmer another 30 minutes, or until tender. Serves 4.

TRAY BOY: *veal steaks, boiling water, onion, salt and pepper, sauterne, cream, flour, sugar, butter*

Menu

cream of leek and potato soup
veal steaks
cabbage, apple, and raisin slaw
baked yams *
hot rolls
baba au rhum
café diable

Barbecued Veal Chops

4 veal chops 1 inch thick

Sauce:
¼ cup oil
2 tablespoons lemon juice
½ teaspoon salt
¼ teaspoon pepper
1 clove garlic mashed
pinch of marjoram
2 tablespoons Worcestershire
    sauce
2 tablespoons catsup

Beforehand Preparation: Mix the barbecue sauce. Place in a bowl.

At the Grill: Place the chops in a hand grill and sear the chops near the coals. Remove to a higher position. Turn and baste with sauce frequently until tender. This should take about 35 minutes. Serve on hot plates with remaining warm barbecue sauce. Serves 4.

TRAY BOY: *chops, sauce*

Menu

seasoned tomato juice
barbecued veal chops
stuffed baked potatoes
toasted hard rolls
molded Bing-cherry salad
red wine or coffee

Veal Roll-Ups

1 pound veal sliced and
    pounded thin
juice of ½ lemon
2 tablespoons butter
3 tablespoons dry breadcrumbs
2 tablespoons chopped chives
1 tablespoon chopped parsley
½ teaspoon marjoram
1 clove garlic, mashed through
    garlic press
dash of freshly ground nutmeg
1 teaspoon salt
¼ teaspoon pepper
2 tablespoons chopped
    luncheon meat
1 tablespoon raisins
2 tablespoons olive oil
2 tablespoons sherry

Sauce:
2 tablespoons sherry
1 teaspoon cornstarch
¼ cup stock

Beforehand Preparation: Sauté chives, breadcrumbs, and parsley in butter for 3 minutes. Add marjoram, garlic, nutmeg, salt, pepper, luncheon meat, and raisins. Mix well. Cut veal into 8 pieces about 3 by 4 inches. Sprinkle with lemon juice. Place a tablespoon of filling on each and roll like a jelly roll. Fasten each end with string.

At the Grill: Brown rolls quickly in hot oil. Add sherry. Cover and simmer for 45 minutes. Add water if necessary. Add the sauce and heat through again. Season. Serves 4.

TRAY BOY: *veal rolls, olive oil, sherry, sauce*

Menu

stuffed celery
veal roll-ups
rice pilau *
grilled tomatoes *
pineapple, coconut, and strawberries in sherry
coffee

Veal Scaloppine Napoli

1½ pounds boneless veal cut
   from leg
¼ cup grated Parmesan cheese
3 tablespoons olive oil
1 cup bouillon
1 mashed clove of garlic

½ cup sherry
½ teaspoon marjoram
¼ teaspoon freshly grated
   nutmeg
flour
¼ teaspoon pepper

Beforehand Preparation: Veal should be cut very thin and beaten with a mallet or flat side of cleaver. Cut in pieces approximately 4 inches square. Rinse and wipe dry. Dredge both sides with cheese.

At the Grill: Heat oil in a skillet. When very hot, add veal and brown quickly. Remove from fire. Add bouillon, garlic, marjoram, nutmeg, pepper, and sherry. Cover and cook slowly until very tender. Turn 3 or 4 times to keep tender, and add water if necessary. Thicken sauce with flour if desired. Cooking time about 30 minutes. Serves 4.

TRAY BOY: *veal, oil, bouillon, sherry, marjoram, nutmeg, garlic, pepper, flour*

Menu

olive and raw vegetable spread *
veal scaloppine Napoli
noodles
zucchini *
fruit salad
iced tea

Scaloppine Sandwiches Supreme

8 thin slices of veal
4 slices ham 1/16-inch thick and
    4 inches square
4 slices of Swiss cheese
flour

pepper
salt
1/3 cup butter or margarine
2 tablespoons sherry

Beforehand Preparation: Get thin, thin slices of veal cut from the leg as uniformly as possible; they should be about 4 inches square. Mix the flour, salt, and pepper.

At the Grill: Make 4 sandwiches of a slice of veal, a slice of ham, a slice of cheese and a slice of veal. Dredge the sandwiches with seasoned flour. Heat the butter or margarine in a skillet and sauté the sandwiches slowly until brown on both sides (about 30 minutes). Sprinkle with sherry a few minutes before serving. Serves 4.

TRAY BOY: *veal, ham, cheese, seasoned flour, margarine, sherry*

Menu

scaloppine sandwiches supreme
garlic bread *
tossed green salad *
homemade ice cream
coffee

Connecticut Veal Stew

2 pounds veal stew meat
1 #2 can tomatoes
3 stalks celery
8 small onions
1 coarsely chopped green
  pepper
1 bunch tiny carrots

1 teaspoon salt
½ teaspoon freshly ground
  pepper
1 bay leaf
6 cloves
parsley

Beforehand Preparation: Remove excess fat from meat and cut into 2-inch cubes. Cut celery into 2-inch pieces. Clean carrots. Parboil onions and pepper strips for 10 minutes. Chop parsley.

At the Grill: Brown meat in hot, dry pan. Add tomatoes, cover. Simmer 20 minutes. Add celery, carrots, salt, pepper, bay leaf, and cloves. Cook for 20 minutes. Add onions and chopped green pepper. Cook 20 minutes more. Green string beans and potato balls may be parboiled and added with onions. Dish into large soup plates. Garnish with chopped parsley. Serves 4.

TRAY BOY: *veal, tomatoes, celery, onions, green peppers, carrots, salt, pepper, bay leaf, clove, parsley*

Menu

veal stew
macaroni salad *
hot buttermilk biscuits
fresh fruit and cheese
coffee

Hungarian Goulash

2 pounds boneless lean veal
    flour
1 cup chopped onion
3 tablespoons drippings
1 tablespoon paprika
1 teaspoon salt
¼ teaspoon freshly ground
    pepper

2 quartered tomatoes
1 tablespoon minced parsley
1 cup bouillon
1 mashed clove of garlic
a pinch thyme
1 stalk celery cut into 1-inch
    pieces

Beforehand Preparation: Cut meat into 2-inch cubes. Chop the vegetables. Roll veal in flour, pressing in as much flour as possible.

At the Grill: Heat Dutch oven. Add drippings, and when sizzling hot add onions and meat. Cook until onions are transparent and meat is browned on all sides. Add salt, paprika, and pepper. Cook 5 minutes. Add parsley, tomatoes, bouillon, garlic, thyme, and celery. Cover tightly and cook for 1½ hours. Add more water from time to time if necessary. Serves 6.

TRAY BOY: *drippings, meat, onions, salt, paprika, pepper mill, parsley, tomatoes, bouillon, garlic, thyme, celery*

Menu

Hungarian goulash
noodles
cole slaw with cream dressing *
pumpernickel bread
fruit compote
beer

Grilled Sweetbreads

3 pairs sweetbreads
2 tablespoons vinegar
¼ cup butter

1 tablespoon lemon juice
salt and pepper to taste

Beforehand Preparation: Trim sweetbreads and parboil in water to cover, adding ½ teaspoon salt and 2 tablespoons vinegar. Let boil gently 30 minutes; take from pan at once and put in cold water. Remove exterior membrane and tissue. Return to water until ready to use.

At the Grill: Cut sweetbreads apart and cut each in two lengthwise. Place on well-buttered wire broiler, close, and broil about 6 minutes, turning three or four times. Have ready 6 slices toast spread with lemon butter (made by creaming ¼ cup butter with 1 tablespoon lemon juice and salt and pepper to taste). Serves 6.

TRAY BOY: *sweetbreads, butter, lemon juice, salt, pepper mill, white bread*

Menu

clear tomato soup
grilled sweetbreads on toast
French-fried potatoes
buttered peas
lettuce-and-tomato salad with Russian dressing
crackers, jam, cheese
demitasse

SERVICE NOTE: *Toast should be made over hot coals, using wire broiler or long toasting forks.*

Savory Tongue

a small tongue, fresh or
  smoked, cooked tender
2 tablespoons butter or oil
2 tablespoons chopped onion
1 mashed clove of garlic
1 chopped green pepper

2 tablespoons flour
1 cup tomato juice
2 cups stock
1 tablespoon vinegar
chili powder
salt and pepper

Beforehand Preparation: Remove skin from tongue and cut into medium-thick slices.

At the Grill: Heat butter or oil in Dutch oven and add onion, garlic, and pepper. Put over fire, and when vegetables are soft, blend in flour and add tomato juice and stock. When smooth add vinegar with chili powder, salt, and pepper to taste. Arrange slices of tongue in Dutch oven, lifting with a fork to cover meat evenly with sauce. Cover the "oven" and simmer gently for about 30 minutes. Serves 6.

TRAY BOY: *tongue slices, butter or oil, chopped onion, garlic, green pepper, flour, tomato juice, stock, vinegar, salt, pepper mill, chili powder*

Menu

tomato juice
savory tongue
roasted potatoes *
chopped spinach with hard-cooked egg
apple and celery salad
cream-cheese, bar-le-duc jelly, crackers
red wine

PORK

The First Recorded Barbecue Concerned an Unfortunate Chinese Roast Pig

Roast Suckling Pig

1 suckling pig about 6 weeks
    old
2 large onions, chopped
4 cups breadcrumbs
1 tablespoon salt
½ teaspoon pepper
½ teaspoon sage

½ teaspoon marjoram
½ cup boiling water
1 cup pineapple juice
flour for gravy
salt
pepper
choice of garnishes

Beforehand Preparation: Select a fine, plump animal about 15 or 20 pounds in weight. Have it dressed for roasting, leaving head intact but removing feet. Boil the heart and liver until tender. Chop them into giblet-size pieces. Sauté onion and add to heart, etc. Season with salt, pepper, sage and marjoram. Add the breadcrumbs and pour over the boiling water. Mix well. Stuff into pig while hot. Sew the opening and carefully truss with greased cord so that the legs are in a kneeling position. Insert a stone or block of wood to hold the mouth open.

At the Grill: Run a sharpened stout skewer through the carcass. Fasten so that it is well-balanced and secure on the skewer. Cook slowly over the coals. Turn constantly and baste with a marinade made of 1 cup hot drippings, 1 cup hot water, and 1 cup pineapple juice. Have a drip pan underneath to catch the juice. Cooking time will be from 5 to 6 hours. The last hour use only the drippings in pan for basting. When cooked, sever the head partially from shoulders.

Place on a large board and gaily dress the pig with an apple in its mouth, bright red cherries in its eyes, and a garland of green parsley round the neck. Decorate the platter very festively with spiced peaches, spiced crabapples, halves of pears filled with mint jelly, etc., to your own liking. Serve hot.

TRAY BOY: *pig, pineapple juice, flour, salt, pepper mill, apple, cherries, parsley, choice of other garnishes*

Menu

minced-clam-and-cream-cheese dunking sauce with celery curls *
roast suckling pig
gravy and fruit garnishes
parsley new potatoes
asparagus
cheese and crackers
coffee

Roast Leg of Pork

leg of pork
celery
sage
salt
pepper
flour for gravy
1 #2 can pears
1 jar currant jelly

Marinade:
½ cup lemon juice
½ cup orange juice
½ cup vinegar
2 cups cider
1 sliced onion
1 mashed clove of garlic
Tabasco sauce

Beforehand Preparation: Have the butcher prepare the leg as usual, but remove the bone. Leave for 12 hours in the marinade.

At the Grill: Sprinkle several stalks of leafy, wet celery with sage, salt and pepper, and stuff them in the bone cavity. Score the pig skin in several places. Arrange securely and evenly on the spit so as to balance correctly, and place over low heat. Allow 30 minutes per pound. Turn constantly, basting with marinade. Have a drip pan below to catch the drippings for gravy. When thoroughly cooked, make the gravy. Garnish the meat platter with canned pears; fill centers with currant jelly. Serve while hot. Figure 2 pounds for 3 people.

TRAY BOY: *celery, sage, salt, pepper mill, leg of pork, flour, pears, currant jelly, marinade*

Menu

stuffed eggs *
roast leg of pork
pears with currant jelly
mashed potatoes and gravy
zucchini *
apple pie * and snappy cheese
coffee

Carnival Pork Steak

1½-pound pork steak (fresh ham)

lard or other fat

flour, salt and pepper as needed

Colorado barbecue sauce * or any other good barbecue sauce

Beforehand Preparation: Get the butcher to cut steaks an inch to two inches thick. Trim off excess fat. Dredge steaks well with seasoned flour.

At the Grill: Melt 2 tablespoons fat in bottom of Dutch oven or heavy skillet. Put in the steak and brown on both sides. Add just enough hot water to barely cover, and let cook slowly until tender. Add 1½ cups barbecue sauce and let simmer a few minutes longer. Season. Place steak on platter with sauce poured over. Serves 6.

TRAY BOY: *pork steak, fat, salt, pepper mill, barbecue sauce*

Menu

oyster or crab bisque
carnival pork steak
fried hominy cakes *
baked or grilled whole onions *
shredded cabbage with Thousand Island dressing
fruit
choice of beverage

Barbecued Sweet and Sour Pork Tenderloin

2 pounds of pork tenderloin
1 tablespoon soya sauce
1½ tablespoons molasses
1 tablespoon vinegar
1 teaspoon MSG

Hot Sauce:
2 tablespoons molasses
1 cup tomato juice
2 tablespoons prepared
    mustard
2 tablespoons vinegar
1 tablespoon soya sauce
¼ teaspoon rosemary
¼ teaspoon curry

Beforehand Preparation: Have your butcher split the tenderloin into 2 pieces lengthwise. Mix the soya sauce, molasses, vinegar and MSG into a paste. Coat the pork with the mixture. Let stand at room temperature for an hour. Mix the ingredients for the sauce. Simmer for five minutes.

At the Grill: Grease the grid of your grill well to prevent sticking. Place the meat on it when the coals are medium. Turn frequently. Cooking time will be about 30 to 45 minutes. Test for doneness. Serve at once with the hot sauce. Serves 4.

TRAY BOY: *tenderloin, hot sauce*

Menu

sweet and sour pork tenderloin
hot sauce
rice *
string beans
Chinese noodles
almond cakes
tea

Barbecued Pork Chops

6 pork chops
seasoned flour
1 small onion
1 clove garlic
1 tablespoon Worcestershire
   sauce

4 tablespoons vinegar
4 tablespoons catsup
3 to 4 drops Tabasco sauce
salt and pepper to taste

Beforehand Preparation: Cut up onion and garlic. Place in small piece of cheesecloth and tie securely. Trim chops of excess fat.

At the Grill: Dredge chops and place in ungreased hot skillet and brown slowly, 5 minutes on each side. Fat left on chops will make greasing skillet unnecessary. Put onion-and-garlic bag in pan, add remaining ingredients with salt and pepper to taste. Cover closely and cook slowly 30 minutes, basting occasionally with sauce. Remove bag. Serves 6.

TRAY BOY: *pork chops, seasoned flour, onion and garlic bag, Worcestershire sauce, vinegar, catsup, Tabasco sauce, salt, pepper mill*

Menu

melon-ball cups with chopped mint
barbecued pork chops
fried hominy *
baked onions
tomato-and-avocado salad
roasted apples * topped with ice cream
coffee

Barbecued Ham Slice

1 large slice of ham 1½ inches
    thick

Marinade:
¼ cup red wine
1 pinch thyme
¼ teaspoon pepper
6 cloves
1 tablespoon corn syrup
2 tablespoons fat

Beforehand Preparation: Make a marinade of the wine, thyme, pepper, cloves, syrup, and fat. Gash the edges of the ham about every ½ inch to prevent curling. Brush both sides with marinade and let stand at room temperature for 2 hours before broiling.

At the Grill: Place the ham steak on the greased grill. Cook slowly, basting with the sauce every few minutes. Brown and turn. When brown on the second side, serve with remaining sauce. Serves 4.

TRAY BOY: *ham, barbecue sauce*

Menu

barbecued ham slice
roasted sweet potatoes *
succotash *
fresh pineapple chunks with mint
iced tea

Ham Steak (Hawaiian)

2 pounds ham steaks 1½ inches thick
2 tablespoons prepared mustard

2 tablespoons brown sugar
½ cup pineapple juice

Beforehand Preparation: Trim the edges of the ham steak and gash about every ½ inch to prevent curling. Parboil in a little water for 5 minutes to remove some of the salt and to tenderize.

At the Grill: Spread both sides of the ham with mustard. Place in a greased skillet. Sprinkle with brown sugar, pour on the pineapple juice. Cook for about 30 minutes, or until tender. Serves 4.

TRAY BOY: *ham steak, mustard, brown sugar, pineapple juice*

Menu

clam-and-cream-cheese dunk *
ham steak
glazed pineapple rings *
celery and cucumber sticks
yams
raspberries and cream
coffee

Glazed Ham Steaks with Apples

2 slices smoked ham ¾-inch
    thick
½ cup dry breadcrumbs
1 cup brown sugar

2 teaspoons dry mustard
1½ cups cider
2 apples

Beforehand Preparation: Make a mixture of crumbs, sugar, and mustard. Parboil ham slices for 5 minutes.

At the Grill: Place ham slices in a large skillet with cover. Spread with seasoned crumbs, pour over the cider. Cover and cook over moderate heat for 30 minutes. Have apples peeled, cored, and sliced ½-inch thick. Turn the ham and cover with apple slices. Baste over all. Add more water if needed. Cook 30 minutes longer. Serves 4.

TRAY BOY: *ham slices, seasoned breadcrumbs, cider, apples*

Menu

grapefruit cocktail
ham slices
broiled pineapple slices *
quick-frozen whipped potatoes
cabbage salad *
apple pie
coffee

Ham with Currant-Wine Sauce

4 ham slices (½-inch thick)
1 tablespoon cornstarch
½ tablespoon dry mustard
1 cup Burgundy
¼ cup light vinegar

2-inch stick cinnamon
½ teaspoon powdered cloves
½ cup small dried currants
½ cup brown sugar

Beforehand Preparation: Soak the currants in wine overnight. Drain off the wine. Mix the dry ingredients together. Add wine, stir in vinegar, and cook until sauce thickens, stirring constantly. Add currants.

At the Grill: Broil ham slices carefully on both sides. Place on separate sizzling platters. Pour heated sauce over each slice. Serve at once. Serves 4.

TRAY BOY: *ham, sauce*

Menu

cheese platter for nibblers *
ham with currant-and-wine sauce
corn on cob *
spider bread *
fruit
coffee

Grilled Ham with an Elegant Mushroom Sauce

2 ham steaks ½-inch thick
3 tablespoons vinegar
1½ teaspoons dry mustard
½ teaspoon sugar

2 tablespoons currant jelly
½ pound mushrooms
butter as needed
salt, pepper, paprika

Beforehand Preparation: Soak ham slices in cold water 30 minutes. Score the fat edges to prevent curling. Peel and slice mushrooms. Put ham in skillet, add a little water, cover and let steam 10 minutes.

At the Grill: Mix vinegar, mustard, sugar, and jelly in saucepan and heat, but do not boil. Broil ham in wire broiler. Sauté mushrooms in butter and combine with sauce. Place broiled ham on a heated platter and pour mushroom sauce over. Salt, pepper, and paprika may be added to sauce if desired. Serves 4.

TRAY BOY: *ham steaks, vinegar, mustard, sugar, jelly, mushrooms, butter, seasonings*

Menu

guacamole with crumbled bacon crackers *
ham with mushrooms
roasted sweet potatoes *
succotash *
apple and celery salad
cola drink

Dutch-Oven Spare Ribs

4 pounds spare ribs
flour, salt, pepper
1 small onion
1 clove garlic
5 tablespoons butter or other
    fat

2 tablespoons catsup
2 or 3 teaspoons vinegar
1 cup water
2 tablespoons A-1 Sauce

Beforehand Preparation: Have ribs cracked by your butcher. Chop onion and mash garlic. Rub seasoned flour into spare ribs.

At the Grill: Heat 3 tablespoons of fat in bottom of Dutch oven; brown floured spare ribs thoroughly on both sides. Take from the oven, put rack in bottom of oven, and then the ribs. Melt 2 tablespoons fat in a small skillet, add onion and garlic. When soft, add catsup, vinegar, water, and A-1 sauce. Salt and pepper to taste. Pour sauce over the ribs, cover closely, and cook until tender, adding a little water if needed. This will take about two hours. Serves 6.

TRAY BOY: *floured spare ribs, onion and garlic, butter or other fat, catsup, vinegar, A-1 Sauce, salt, pepper mill*

Menu

    pineapple juice with shredded mint
    Dutch-oven spare ribs
    savory kidney beans
    brown bread
    green peppers filled with cream cheese and nuts
    charlotte russe
    coffee

SERVICE NOTE: *Charlotte russe is a good choice for your outdoor meal, as the cream can be whipped just before serving. Flavor with vanilla or rum if desired.*

Barbecued Spare Ribs

3 pounds of spare ribs
salt
freshly ground pepper

Sauce:
1 tablespoon bacon fat
1 medium onion chopped
½ cup tomato juice
juice of 1 lemon
2 tablespoons brown sugar
1 tablespoon Worcestershire
    sauce
1 cup chili sauce
1 dash of Tabasco sauce

Beforehand Preparation: Have the spare ribs cracked down the middle and cut into 6-inch pieces. Make the sauce by browning the onions in the fat, adding the other ingredients, and simmering for 20 minutes.

At the Grill: Sprinkle the ribs with salt and pepper. Broil over slow heat for 30 minutes; turn and baste often. Test for absolute doneness before serving. Serve with the remaining sauce. Serves 4.

TRAY BOY: *spare ribs, salt, pepper, barbecue sauce*

Menu

raw vegetable platter for nibblers *
barbecued spare ribs and sauce
hot potato chips
bread-and-butter sandwiches
fruit compote
coffee

Hickory-Flavored Spare Ribs

3 pounds spare ribs
Charcrust
1 teaspoon curry powder
1 mashed clove of garlic
2 tablespoons onion juice

Sauce:
½ cup white wine
2 tablespoons water
⅛ teaspoon rosemary
½ teaspoon ginger
⅛ teaspoon black pepper
2 tablespoons catsup

Beforehand Preparation: Have spare ribs cracked down center and cut into convenient pieces. Mix garlic, curry powder and onion juice to a paste. Spread over meat. Sprinkle generously with Charcrust and allow to stand at room temperature for several hours. Mix ingredients of basting sauce. Bring to a boil and simmer 5 minutes.

At the Grill: Place directly on grill. Turn often. Baste with each turn. Test for doneness in about 20 minutes. There should be no pink meat in the thickest part. Serves 4.

TRAY BOY: *seasoned spare ribs, basting sauce, Charcrust*

Menu

popcorn *
hickory-flavored spare ribs
hashed brown potatoes *
stuffed-tomato salad
brownies and ice cream
beer

Spare Ribs South of the Border

3 pounds spare ribs
1 can (10 oz.) tomato sauce
1 small onion chopped fine
1 stalk celery chopped fine
1 mashed clove of garlic
2 dashes of Tabasco sauce
2 tablespoons A-1 sauce

2 tablespoons red wine vinegar
1/4 teaspoon powdered clove
1/4 teaspoon cinnamon
1 tablespoon sugar
1/2 teaspoon chili powder
2 tablespoons chutney
1/8 teaspoon dry mustard

Beforehand Preparation: Buy lean ribs. Leave them in one piece. Mix all the other ingredients together. Bring to a boil and simmer slowly for 30 minutes, stirring occasionally.

At the Grill: Place the ribs on the grill and turn every seven minutes, basting with the sauce. They will take 30 to 45 minutes, depending on heat and size, but test to be sure the pork is cooked thoroughly. Serve with remaining sauce. Serves 4.

TRAY BOY: *spare ribs, barbecue sauce*

Menu

spare ribs
barbecue sauce
vegetable-slaw salad
salty rye bread, sliced thin
cheesecake
beer or ale

Creole Sausage Grill

3 pounds medium-lean pork
1 onion
1 clove garlic
2 teaspoons salt

½ teaspoon thyme
½ teaspoon powdered bay leaf
dash allspice
chili pepper

Beforehand Preparation: Have butcher grind the pork. Put into large bowl, add other ingredients, and mix well. Form into cakes, place on waxed paper, and leave in refrigerator until needed.

At the Grill: Put the sausage cakes in slightly greased griddle and brown first on one side and then on the other, flattening out with spatula so that they will cook through. When done, place on platter, pour off excess fat from griddle, add a few tablespoons boiling water, stir to take up drippings, and pour over sausages. Sprinkle with additional salt and pepper to taste. Serves 6.

TRAY BOY: *sausage cakes, pepper, salt*

Menu

tangerine juice
sausage cakes
flapjacks * and syrup
campfire coffee *

SERVICE NOTE: *Home-mixed sausage meat is definitely a conversation piece. Ready-made link sausages that don't shrink too much are very good over an open fire. Turn often and cook about 20 minutes.*

The Sweetest Meat of All

Barbecued Chicken à la Gloria Swanson

Chicken broiled beneath the open sky is something special, something extra-delicious.

4 small broilers, split in
    quarters
1 clove garlic
⅓ tablespoon cooking oil

Sauce:
2 cups canned tomatoes
1 cup bouillon
2 tablespoons minced onion
½ cup white wine
1 tablespoon Worcestershire
    sauce
½ teaspoon dry mustard
1 teaspoon salt
¼ teaspoon pepper
½ teaspoon chili powder
2 tablespoons butter

Beforehand Preparation: Wipe broilers with a clean, damp cloth. Rub with garlic, then oil. Mix the ingredients for sauce. Bring to a boil and simmer for 15 minutes.

At the Grill: Place chickens on grill. Brown the inside, then the outside. Transfer to a giant steel skillet. Pour sauce over the chickens. Turn frequently during cooking, which should take 35 minutes. Serves 8.

TRAY BOY: *chickens, sauce*

Menu

barbecued chicken à la Gloria Swanson
fluffy rice *
bread-and-butter sandwiches *
cole slaw with cream dressing *
fresh blueberry cobbler
root beer

Barbecued Whole Chicken on a Spit

a 4-pound roasting chicken
3 stalks celery
salt and pepper
¼ teaspoon poultry seasoning

Sauce:
½ teaspoon MSG
½ cup water
¼ cup oil
2 tablespoons lemon juice
½ teaspoon marjoram
1 tablespoon sugar
1 teaspoon salt
1 teaspoon ground juniper
    berries

Beforehand Preparation: Wipe chicken with a damp cloth. Mix and heat barbecue sauce and pour over chicken. Spoon the sauce inside and over the chicken several times while it is standing at room temperature for 30 minutes. Remove from sauce and sprinkle a few stalks of celery with salt, pepper and poultry seasoning.

At the Grill: Using a hand grill or strong long-handled fork, sear the chicken all over near the coals. When browned, place on spit and secure. Turn every 8 minutes, basting with the sauce. The whole cooking time will be from 45 minutes to an hour. Test by pulling leg. If it pulls away easily and there is no red blood inside, the chicken is done. The juniper berries will give the meat a subtle pheasant-like flavor.

TRAY BOY: *chicken, basting sauce*

Menu

barbecued chicken
rice pilau *
zucchini *
hot rolls
honeydew melon
iced tea

Clay Chicken

a broiling chicken with
    feathers
1 piece of bacon
salt

giblets, if desired
1 stalk celery
1 small sliced onion

Beforehand Preparation: The chicken should be drawn and cleaned without removing the feathers. Rub inside with salt. Put a slice of bacon inside. Stuff with celery and onion and chopped seasoned giblets.

At the Grill: Cover chicken with 1-inch thickness of wet clay or mud, being careful to cover the opening with feathers. Bury in a bed of hot ashes and cover with coals. Cook 1 hour. Feathers and skin come off with clay. The meat is more tender than any cookstove can make it. An excellent method of cooking game birds and fish on a camping trip. Serves 2.

TRAY BOY: *prepared chicken*

Menu

clay chicken
hashed brown potatoes *
skillet biscuits *
peas and butter
watercress-and-orange salad
campfire coffee *

Hunter's Fowl (Borrowed from the Italians)

a 4-pound roasting chicken
2 stalks celery
1 large onion
1 cup dry white wine
starch or flour

Dressing:
6 small white onions
½ cup celery, cut in 2-inch
  pieces
1 chopped small green pepper
chopped giblets
2 tablespoons melted
  margarine
2 tablespoons green herbs
  (parsley, chives, tarragon, or
  basil)
½ teaspoon pepper
1 teaspoon salt

Beforehand Preparation: Place dressing ingredients in a bowl and mix. Stuff chicken and truss.

At the Grill: Brown both sides of the chicken on the grill. Remove and place chicken, breast down, on a rack in a Dutch oven. Add celery stalks and chopped onion. Pour in 1 cup water and 1 cup dry white wine. Cover tightly and simmer for 1 hour. Add more water if necessary. Turn fowl over and continue cooking for another hour. Sliced mushrooms may be added to liquid during last 15 minutes. Thicken gravy with starch or flour, if desired. Serves 6.

TRAY BOY: *stuffed chicken, celery, onion, wine, mushrooms (if desired), starch or flour*

Menu

raw-vegetable snack tray *
hunter's fowl
buttered noodles
bread sticks
fresh peach ice cream
spritzer

Blushing Broilers

2 young chickens, about 3
   pounds each
1 teaspoon salt
¼ teaspoon pepper
1 tablespoon paprika
1 tablespoon sugar
2 tablespoons chopped onion

1 cup tomato puree
⅓ cup margarine
½ cup water
1 tablespoon Worcestershire
   sauce
1 tablespoon lemon juice

Beforehand Preparation: Cut chickens in quarters. Put on rack in roasting pan with a little water in bottom, cover closely, and cook in moderate oven until about half done. Chop onion and squeeze lemon. Mix salt, pepper, paprika, and sugar in saucepan. Add onion, tomato puree, margarine, and water, and boil 3 or 4 minutes. Then add lemon juice and Worcestershire sauce.

At the Grill: Place partly cooked chickens in large skillet or Dutch oven, pour sauce over them, cover and let cook 30 minutes or until tender. Remove cover and baste from time to time, adding a little more water if needed. Pour sauce over chicken when serving. Serves 6.

TRAY BOY: *partly cooked chickens, sauce*

Menu

celery stuffed with cream cheese
ripe olives
blushing broilers
wild rice *
peas
romaine salad with French dressing
café parfait
coffee

Savory Broiled Young Chicken

3 2-pound broilers cut in
   halves
1 teaspoon salt
½ teaspoon pepper
½ teaspoon MSG
1 tablespoon honey
1 tablespoon lemon juice

Basting Sauce:
½ teaspoon rosemary
½ teaspoon basil
½ teaspoon chives
½ cup oil
3 tablespoons soy sauce
⅔ cup water

Beforehand Preparation: Wash and dry chickens, rub with a mixture of salt, pepper, MSG, honey, and lemon juice. MSG always amplifies the delicious flavor of chicken. Mix and heat basting sauce.

At the Grill: Place the chickens near the hot coals to sear; always brown inside first. When nicely browned, move further from heat. Turn often and baste frequently with sauce. Let the chickens cook slowly for about 25 minutes or until done. When done there should be no red blood inside. Serves 6.

TRAY BOY: *chickens, basting sauce*

Menu

    green onions, celery, radishes
    savory broiled young chicken
    potatoes hashed in cream
    watercress and romaine salad
    hot biscuits
    fresh strawberries in kirsch
    coffee

Perfect Fried Chicken

2 small fryers cut in pieces
1½ cups flour
2 teaspoons paprika
2 teaspoons salt
½ teaspoon pepper
2 cups bacon fat or shortening
giblets
a pinch of poultry seasoning

Beforehand Preparation: Wash the chicken and wipe dry. Place the flour, paprika, poultry seasoning, salt, and pepper in a strong bag. Drop chicken pieces in, two at a time. Shake bag until they are well coated. Place on a large plate or platter. Save leftover flour for gravy. Put giblets, neck, and wing tips on to simmer. Cook 1 hour.

At the Grill: Use a heavy skillet. Heat the fat until a drop of water will sizzle. Brown largest pieces first. It will take two shifts in a 10-inch skillet to do 2 chickens. Use two skillets and double the fat if convenient. As soon as all chicken is browned, slip an asbestos pad under skillet to reduce heat. Cover, turn several times, and cook until tender, about 30 minutes. Water may be added if cover is not good and tight. Pour out some of the fat and brown 3 tablespoons seasoned flour. Add 2 cups of chicken stock from giblets and cook until creamy. Add chopped giblets. Serves 6.

TRAY BOY: *fat, chicken, seasoned flour, chicken stock, giblets*

Menu

vichyssoise
perfect fried chicken
candied sweet potatoes
minted green peas
beaten biscuits
Bing cherries molded in port wine
coffee

Sherry Chicken Special

Mrs. George C. Kellogg, Oakland, California

1 3½-pound fryer cut in pieces
1 teaspoon seasoned salt
½ teaspoon MSG
¼ teaspoon freshly ground
   pepper
¼ teaspoon paprika
2 cups flour

½ cup margarine
¼ cup shortening
1 small can mushrooms and
   pieces
1 cup dry sherry
1 cup milk

Beforehand Preparation: Wash and dry chicken. Mix seasoned salt, MSG, pepper, paprika, and flour in a paper bag. Drop chicken pieces in two at a time, and shake until well-coated.

At the Grill: Heat Dutch oven, add shortening and margarine. Brown chicken slowly. Add mushrooms, sherry, and milk. Remove to low heat and cook ½ hour.

TRAY BOY: *shortening, margarine, chicken, sherry, milk, mushrooms*

Menu

shrimp remoulade *
sherry chicken special
skillet string beans and onions *
southern biscuits
tossed green salad with Roquefort dressing *
honeydew halves filled with fresh fruit *
spritzer

SERVICE NOTE: *Veal can be prepared in the identical manner.*

Italian Chicken Fricassee

1 4-pound young chicken, jointed
1 teaspoon salt
¼ teaspoon pepper
3 tablespoons flour
1 tablespoon starch
1 tablespoon oil
1 tablespoon butter or margarine
1¼ cups dry white wine
¼ pound shredded pre-cooked ham
1 teaspoon tarragon

Beforehand Preparation: Mix the salt, pepper, and flour. Roll the pieces of chicken in this.

At the Grill: Melt the butter and oil in skillet. Add the floured chicken. Brown thoroughly on all sides. Add wine, ham, and tarragon. Cook slowly, covered, until chicken is done, about 45 minutes. Remove chicken to a warm platter. Thicken sauce in pan with starch mixed well with cold water. Scrape and stir. Cook 3 to 4 minutes. Serves 4.

TRAY BOY: *chicken, butter, oil, wine, ham, tarragon*

Menu

antipasti *
Italian chicken fricassee with pan gravy
fluffy hot rice *
garlic bread *
dandelion salad
fresh fruit and cheese
coffee

Coq au Vin (French style chicken fricassee)

1 4- to 5-pound chicken
fat
salt
pepper
4 ounces of oil
¼ cup brandy
1 clove garlic

1 bay leaf
⅛ teaspoon thyme
2 teaspoons chopped parsley
12 small white onions
18 small mushroom caps
¼ pound ham in ½-inch cubes
1 cup red wine

Beforehand Preparation: Cut chicken in pieces for frying.

At the Grill: Sprinkle the chicken with salt and pepper and wipe with fat. Sear in a hand grill over hot coals until the chicken is completely golden brown all over. Take care not to scorch it. Now start the Dutch-oven operation. Heat the pot, pour in the oil. When it is sizzling hot, add the chicken. Pour on brandy and set ablaze. After a few minutes, extinguish the flame. Crush a clove of garlic through the garlic press over the chicken. Add bay leaf, thyme, and parsley. Cover. Cook for 15 minutes. Add the onions, mushrooms, ham, and wine. Cover for a few minutes and season with salt and pepper to taste. Cover again and cook until the chicken is very tender. Serves 6.

TRAY BOY: *chicken, salt, pepper mill, fat, oil, brandy, garlic, bay leaf, thyme, parsley, onions, mushroom caps, ham, wine*

Menu

vichyssoise
coq au vin
potato balls with parsley
tossed salad *
rhubarb tarts
coffee with brandy

Devil's Bones

6 chicken drumsticks or second joints
seasoned flour
1½ cups chicken stock
3 tablespoons butter
2 tablespoons chili sauce
½ teaspoon Worcestershire sauce
1 teaspoon prepared mustard
salt and pepper

Beforehand Preparation: Simmer chicken drumsticks or second joints in just enough water to cover. When tender take from pan and add water to provide 1½ cups liquid, using a chicken cube if needed. Cut three or four gashes in each piece of chicken, roll in seasoned flour, and place on plate.

At the Grill: Heat butter in a skillet and fry chicken parts until nicely browned. Place on dish and keep hot. Add chili sauce, Worcestershire sauce and mustard, salt and pepper to taste, to the stock. Blend and cook 4 or 5 minutes. Return chicken to the pot, mix with sauce, heat through, and serve. Serves 6.

TRAY BOY: *floured chicken pieces, chicken stock, margarine, chili sauce, Worcestershire sauce, mustard, salt, pepper mill*

Menu

jellied tomato madrilene
devil's bones
brown rice
baby limas
cottage-cheese-and-endive salad
macedoine of fruit
coffee

SERVICE NOTE: *Chicken parts can be bought at many poultry stores. For hearty fare allow two pieces for each service. Use hotter seasoning if desired by adding a dash of Tabasco sauce*

Brunswick Stew

a hen, jointed †
2 lbs. boneless rump or shank veal †
¼ cup drippings
1 cup onions
4 cups boiling water
1 #2½ can tomatoes
3 cups of fresh corn kernels
2 cups raw lima beans

1 cup cut okra
1 tablespoon Worcestershire sauce
1 teaspoon chili powder
1 teaspoon powdered cloves
2 teaspoons salt
½ teaspoon pepper
1 teaspoon Tabasco sauce
¼ lb. butter

Beforehand Preparation: Chop vegetables. Cut veal in large chunks. Sauté the cut okra 5 minutes.

At the Grill: Sauté the meat in drippings in a heavy pot until brown all over. Remove meat and sauté the onions until they begin to take on color. Pour in boiling water and cook until the meat is very tender and chicken falls from the bone. Remove all bones. Add tomatoes slowly. Be careful to stir all the time. Scorching will ruin the whole stew. Add vegetables, Worcestershire sauce, chili powder, cloves, salt, pepper, and Tabasco sauce. Cook until the vegetables are tender—about one hour longer. Add butter; now the stew should be slightly liquid, but thick enough to eat with a fork. Use your discretion about thickening or thinning at this point. Add bread crumbs or water if necessary. Correct seasoning. Serve very hot. Serves 8. Brunswick stew is a Georgia barbecue dish and an all-day affair, so plan to start in the morning with plenty of fuel.

TRAY BOY: *chicken, veal, drippings, onions, tomatoes, corn, lima beans, okra, Worcestershire sauce, chili powder, cloves, salt, pepper, Tabasco sauce, butter*

Menu

vegetable platter for nibblers *
Brunswick stew
hot biscuits
pecan pie
beer or ale

† Rabbit, squirrel, lamb, or pork may be used; depending on your farmer's supply.

Prairie Steamer

3 young chickens cut in eighths
18 small potatoes
12 small onions

12 sausages (optional)
as many ears of corn as the
    crowd can eat

Beforehand Preparation: Pluck the chickens, scrub the potatoes, peel the onions and husk the corn.

At the Grill: Spread a thick layer of corn husks on the bottom of a wash tub or a large kettle. Pour in one quart of water. Spread a layer of scrubbed potatoes in jackets and peeled onions next. Cover with corn husks. Now add a layer of chicken parts and sausages. Add another layer of corn husks and the ears of corn. Cover with a blanket of corn husks. Top with one potato (when it is done, everything else will be cooked). Cover the pot and steam over a wood or charcoal fire for 1½ hours. The blend of flavors is straight from heaven.

SERVICE NOTE: *This is a wonderful way to feed a crowd of people in the open. Have a large basket of bread and butter sandwiches, salt and pepper shakers and relishes on the table. A huge pot of campfire coffee and slices of chilled watermelon will fill the bill. Then gather the crowd around the campfire and have a wonderful old-fashioned song fest, and your guests will remember the prairie steamer day as a special event in their lives.*

Chicken Burdwan (an East Indian recipe)

a 4-pound chicken, quartered
3 cups water or stock
12 green onions with tops
1 tablespoon anchovy paste
¼ teaspoon cayenne pepper
2 tablespoons butter

2 tablespoons flour
¾ cup chow-chow pickles
¼ teaspoon chili powder
1 teaspoon salt
1 cup sherry
2 limes cut in wedges

Beforehand Preparation: Parboil the chicken 5 minutes in water or stock. Save the broth. Mince the onion tops, leaving the white bulbs intact. Cut the pickles into ½-inch squares. Blend flour and butter.

At the Grill: Use a Dutch oven with a cover for this. Pour in 1 cup of the chicken broth. Add the onion greens, anchovy paste, and cayenne pepper. Bring to a boil. Drop the flour-and-butter mixture into the sauce. Add the onion bulbs, pickles, chili powder, and salt. Bring to a boil again. Add the fowl and sherry. Simmer covered for 20 minutes. Serve with lime. Serves 6.

TRAY BOY: *chicken, broth, onions and greens, anchovy paste, cayenne pepper, butter and flour, pickles, chili powder, salt, sherry, lime wedges*

Menu

chicken Burdwan
saffron rice *
sliced tomatoes
toast
brandied peaches and wafers
tea

Whole Roast Turkey Cooked on a Spit

turkey weighing 15-18 pounds
giblets
1 cup of fat
flour
salt
pepper
celery salt

Dressing:
4 pounds stale bread
1 cup of margarine
1 cup of finely chopped onion
⅓ cup chopped celery
1 teaspoon pepper
2½ teaspoons salt
1 tablespoon poultry seasoning
1 teaspoon powdered sage

Beforehand Preparation: Prepare and stuff the turkey as for oven roasting. Truss with care. Cook the giblets for gravy. Save the giblet stock.

At the Grill: Fasten the bird on the spit very securely. Turn every 10 or 15 minutes, basting with fat. Place a drip pan under the bird to catch the drippings and use them for gravy mixings. Roasting time will take from 3½ to 4 hours. Test the leg, and when it pulls easily from the carcass the bird is done. Add flour to the drippings and mix in sufficient flour and giblet stock. Season. When this reaches the desired consistency add the cooked chopped giblets. Serves 20.

TRAY BOY: *stuffed turkey, fat, giblets and stock, flour, salt, pepper, celery salt*

Menu

roast turkey with stuffing
gravy
cranberry sauce
mashed potatoes
hot rolls and butter
peas cooked in mushroom soup
pumpkin pie
coffee

SERVICE NOTE: *For Brazil-nut or chestnut stuffing, eliminate the celery, cut the bread to 3 pounds, and add 2 cups of nuts. For oyster stuffing use the same recipe, cutting bread to 3 pounds, and using only ⅓ cup of onion. Add 1 pint of drained oysters and 3 tablespoons of minced parsley.*

Lemon-Barbecued Small Turkey

1 small turkey (4 to 6 pounds)
1 teaspoon salt
1 teaspoon sugar
⅛ teaspoon freshly ground
   pepper

¼ teaspoon paprika
3 tablespoons melted fat
2 lemons

Beforehand Preparation: Have turkey split in half lengthwise. Break the joints of the drumsticks, hip and wing. Skewer the legs and wings into position. Rub both sides of turkey pieces with cut lemon, squeezing lemon to obtain plenty of juice. Brush with melted fat. Sprinkle with a mixture of salt, freshly ground pepper, paprika, and sugar.

At the Grill: Place the turkey halves in a large double-hinged rack and roast slowly for about an hour. Turn every 15 minutes, brushing with melted fat each time. The turkey is done when the meat on the thickest part of the drumstick cuts easily and there is no pink color visible. Serves 8.

TRAY BOY: *prepared turkey halves, can of melted fat and brush*

Menu

cranberry-juice cocktail
lemon-barbecued turkey
scalloped sweet potatoes
French string beans
watercress-and-orange salad
mints
salted nuts
coffee

Squab in Sour Cream

4 squabs
½ teaspoon powdered thyme
1 teaspoon onion salt
⅓ cup butter
fine bread crumbs
¼ cup shortening

2 green onions and tops
2 tomatoes
1 cup white wine
½ cup grated cheese
1 cup sour cream

Beforehand Preparation: Have the birds split. Mix the thyme and onion salt. Rub it on the birds, inside and out. Melt the butter and coat the birds with it. Dust lightly with crumbs. Mince the onions; skin and mince the tomatoes.

At the Grill: Melt the shortening in a large skillet. Brown the birds in this. Add onion, tomatoes, and wine. Cover and cook 30 minutes, turning the birds several times. Just before they are done sprinkle with the cheese. When done remove the squabs to a warm platter. Add the sour cream to the sauce in the pan. Remove from heat. Mix well and serve at once around the birds. Serves 4.

TRAY BOY: *squabs, shortening, onions, tomatoes, wine, cheese, sour cream*

Menu

barbecued cocktail sausages, chicken livers, etc., on
  skewers *
squab in sour cream
wild rice *
tossed green salad *
biscuit tortoni
white wine

Guinea Hen à La Grillade

2 medium-sized guinea hens

Marinade:
½ cup olive oil
1 teaspoon salt
3 teaspoons grapefruit juice
3 tablespoons white wine
    vinegar
2 tablespoons catsup
1 slice onion
¼ teaspoon black pepper
¼ teaspoon sugar
½ teaspoon marjoram

Beforehand Preparation: Have butcher dress hens for broiling, cutting tendons at joints. Birds should be split on breast side but left in one piece. Clean thoroughly and place in a glass dish. Mix remaining ingredients, pour over birds as a marinade, and let stand 8 or 10 hours, turning occasionally.

At the Grill: Lift hens from marinade and place on well-greased wire broiler with bone side exposed to fire first. Close broiler and broil over fire. Turn and baste several times to insure even cooking. Heat marinade, but do not boil. Place birds on serving dish and pour over the sauce. When birds are done they will be brown and tender.

TRAY BOY: *guinea hens in marinade, fat for greasing broiler*

Menu

minced-clam-and-cream-cheese dunking sauce with celery
    sticks *
guinea hen à la grillade
rice pilau with nuts *
asparagus tips with hollandaise sauce
orange sherbet
coffee

Charcoal-Broiled Venison

6 chops ¾ inch thick *or*
1 steak ¾ inch thick
1 clove of garlic
salt

pepper
1 tablespoon oil
1 cup currant jelly
⅓ cup sherry

Beforehand Preparation: Venison should be hung at least 1 week, but preferably 3 or 4 weeks. Broiling and roasting are decidedly superior methods of preparation. The choicest portions are hindquarter and saddle. Wipe the chops or steak. Rub with a cut clove of garlic. Season with salt and pepper.

At the Grill: Place the meat in a hot oiled skillet and broil for 4 minutes on each side. Pour the sherry and jelly over the steak and simmer for a few minutes. Place on hot plates and pour sauce over meat. Serves 6.

TRAY BOY: *chops or steak, oil, currant jelly, sherry*

Menu

artichokes vinaigrette
venison with currant-and-sherry sauce
wild rice *
asparagus tips
finger rolls
pastry
coffee

Venison Perfection

3 pounds aged venison steak
1 tablespoon salt
¼ teaspoon pepper
butter
1 cup tart plum jelly

1 tablespoon cider
2 whole cloves
2 strips orange peel
dash of cinnamon
2 oranges cut in ½-inch slices

Beforehand Preparation: Sprinkle steak with salt and pepper.

At the Grill: Melt 1 tablespoon butter or margarine in saucepan, add jelly, cider, cloves, orange peel, and cinnamon and simmer slowly. Meanwhile brush venison steak with melted butter, place on wire broiler, and broil over brisk fire. It will take 5 or 6 minutes for each side. When done, place on serving platter and pour sauce over, taking care to remove cloves. Garnish with orange slices. Serves 4.

TRAY BOY: venison steak, butter or margarine, jelly, cider, cloves, cinnamon, orange peel and slices

Menu

tomato-and-caviar canapé
venison steak
brown rice and mushroom pilau
green beans
tossed salad *
assorted fresh fruit
cheese, crackers
campfire coffee

Venison Pot Roast

1 saddle of venison 4 inches
    thick
oil
1 clove garlic
½ cup cider
1 cup boiling consommé
1 sliced carrot
1 sliced onion

1 teaspoon salt
½ teaspoon freshly ground
    pepper
½ teaspoon basil
½ teaspoon thyme
½ teaspoon ground clove
4 slices bacon
1 tablespoon flour

Beforehand Preparation: Mash a clove of garlic and rub over the meat thoroughly. Rub with oil. Heat consommé.

At the Grill: Place the roast on the grill near the coals. Sear the roast all over. Return grill to regular cooking position. Pour the liquids and seasonings into a Dutch oven and bring to a boil. Add the meat and vegetables. Lay bacon on top of the meat. Cover and simmer for 1½ hours. Remove meat, skim off fat, and add flour to thicken. Serves 6.

TRAY BOY: *venison, cider, boiling consommé, carrot, onion, salt and pepper, basil, thyme, and clove, bacon, flour*

Menu

celery stuffed with Roquefort cheese
venison pot roast
currant jelly
pan-browned potatoes
glazed carrot sticks
cherry pie
red wine

Fried Rabbit with Cream Gravy

2 young rabbits
¾ cup bacon fat
1 sliced onion
¼ teaspoon allspice
lemon
⅔ cup milk

salt
pepper
flour
1 cup sour cream
watercress

Beforehand Preparation: Have your butcher hang the rabbits for several days. Order them cut into small pieces like a frying chicken. Wipe them with a damp cloth. Rub all over with lemon juice, squeezing the lemon to get all the juice. Sprinkle with salt and pepper. Dip in milk. Roll in flour.

At the Grill: Heat the fat in a skillet. Brown the rabbit. Add onion and allspice. Cover skillet and simmer for an hour, turning every 15 minutes. Remove the rabbit pieces to brown paper to drain. Keep warm. Thicken the juice in the pan with a tablespoon of flour. Add 1 cup of sour cream; simmer for a few minutes. Serve over the rabbit. Garnish with watercress. Serves 6 to 8.

TRAY BOY: *rabbit, bacon fat, onion, allspice, flour, sour cream, watercress*

Menu

cranberry-juice cocktail
fried rabbit with cream gravy
fluffy mashed potatoes
green peas and onion
baking-powder biscuits
spumoni
coffee

Broiled Young Rabbit

2 plump young rabbits
oil

Sauce:
1 teaspoon salt
1 teaspoon pepper
3 tablespoons oil
2 tablespoons lemon juice
a pinch of sage
½ teaspoon garlic salt

Beforehand Preparation: Have your butcher hang the rabbits for several days. Split them and pound them flat so that they will be easy to broil. Mix the sauce.

At the Grill: Brush the rabbit halves with oil and place them on a hand grill. Sear over hot coals until both sides are brown. Raise the grill and broil slowly for about 25 minutes. Baste frequently with the sauce. Turn often. Test to be sure there is no redness to the meat. Serves 6-8.

TRAY BOY: *rabbits, oil, sauce*

Menu

broiled young rabbit
new potatoes in jackets
cornbread
lima beans
blueberry pie
beer

Grilled Quail

4 quail

4 slices bacon

salt

pepper

4 stalks celery and leaves

1 onion sliced

Beforehand Preparation: Clean the birds. Rub inside and out with a mixture of salt and pepper. Place a stalk of celery and a couple of slices of onion inside each bird. Wrap with bacon and secure with small skewers.

At the Grill: Place the birds in a hand grill and sear quickly. Turn often to brown all over. Be careful not to pierce the birds, or the juices will escape. When well-browned, reduce heat and broil slowly for 15 minutes, or until cooked through. Serves 4.

TRAY BOY: *quail wrapped in bacon*

Menu

spiced-shrimp hors d'oeuvres

grilled quail

wild rice *

Brussels sprouts and chestnuts en casserole

mixed green salad *

Poona cheese   toasted crackers

coffee

Broiled Pheasant

1 pheasant
½ cup olive oil
½ cup tarragon white wine
    vinegar

¼ teaspoon pepper
1 teaspoon salt

Beforehand Preparation: Cut the bird into 4 parts and marinate in oil, vinegar, salt, and pepper for four hours.

At the Grill: Place in hand grill and sear quickly. Turn often to brown all over. When well-browned, raise the grill and cook slowly, basting often (about 35 minutes). Test for doneness. Serves 4.

TRAY BOY: *pheasant, marinade*

Menu

marinated mushrooms *
broiled pheasant
rice pilau with giblets *
broccoli vinaigrette
fruit, cheese, and crackers
Rhine wine

Roast Pheasant Supreme

2 pheasants
giblets
1 cup dry sherry
1 cup water
¼ pound melted butter
1 tablespoon flour
½ cup chopped mushrooms

Dressing:
1 finely chopped onion
3 cups bread crumbs
1 teaspoon salt
⅛ teaspoon freshly ground
   pepper
¼ teaspoon marjoram
2 tablespoons melted butter
3 tablespoons water

Beforehand Preparation: Stuff the pheasants with dressing. Truss well. Cook and chop the giblets. Make a basting mixture of sherry, boiling water, and melted butter.

At the Grill: Secure birds on a spit over a drip pan and revolve slowly for about 1 hour, basting every 10 minutes. Test for doneness. Remove to a hot platter. Keep warm. Mix flour and a few tablespoons of pan liquid to a smooth liquid; then stir in remaining pan liquid. Season. Add giblets and mushrooms; stir continuously over low heat 5 or 6 minutes until gravy is of proper thickness. Serve pheasant and gravy separately. Serves 6.

TRAY BOY: *pheasants, basting sauce, flour, salt, pepper mill, giblets, mushrooms*

Menu

onion soup with grated parmesean cheese *
pheasants and gravy
grilled bananas *
broccoli with hollandaise
plum jam
hot muffins
Waldorf salad
white wine

Wild Duck Cooked on a Spit

2 wild ducks
1 apple or orange
1 teaspoon salt
¼ teaspoon freshly ground
   pepper

3 tablespoons oil
4 tablespoons melted butter
4 tablespoons orange juice
1 tablespoon chopped parsley

Beforehand Preparation: Stuff the ducks with pieces of apple or orange. Sprinkle with salt and pepper; rub with oil. Truss well.

At the Grill: Place over the spit. Turn frequently and baste with oil. Cook about 20 minutes, or until blood will not run when meat is pricked. It is a gastronomical crime to overcook wild duck. Remove fruit. Pour melted butter mixed with orange juice and parsley over ducks. Serves 4.

TRAY BOY: *ducks, oil, melted butter, orange juice, parsley*

Menu

celery hearts, colossal olives
wild ducks
wild rice *
plum jelly
string beans with mushrooms
cream cheese and bar-le-duc
red wine

SKEWER METHODS

With Kebabs and Shashlik

Kebab Roundup

Kebabs spell good eating, colorful novelty, and, best of all, ways to serve a large number of guests with a minimum of trouble. Outdoor appetites will make a chef of every guest. Resourceful gourmets will discover endless combinations to string on their wooden-handled spears, alternating the delicate morsels so that the juices and flavors will mingle during the cooking.

The following is an extensive list of possibilities to choose from. Make your selection from the available market offerings with a small or varied spread to suit the occasion.

† 1″ cubes of lamb
† 1″ cubes of beef
1″ squares of thin pre-cooked
    ham

1″ cubes of pre-cooked ham
chicken liver halves (marinate
    in salted milk)
bacon squares

† scallops
† shrimp
oysters

canned crab chunks
clams
† fresh lobster chunks

† mushroom caps
† 1″ squares of green pepper
† 1″ squares of celery
† tiny pearl onions
† 1″ squares of eggplant

½″ discs of cucumber
tomato wedges
tiny red or green tomatoes
½″ discs of zucchini
1″ squares of Bermuda onion

† Marinate in French dressing for several hours before cooking.

bananas, whole or 2″ lengths
pineapple wedges, fresh or
    canned
preserved figs
prunes (may be stuffed with
    cream cheese)

coconut squares
whole apples
whole pears
whole pitted peaches
whole pitted apricots

The small pieces of fruit may be grilled just as they are, or may be marinated in a combination of fruit juice and honey for ½ hour before cooking, then brushed with melted butter. The whole fruits should be speared and cooked until soft. They may then be peeled, sprinkled with brown sugar, and caramelized over the fire. Small pieces of fruit wrapped in bacon and broiled are delicious.

Have the food artistically arranged on large platters garnished with parsley or watercress. Count your skewers to be sure that you have one for each guest. Each person will then alternate meats and vegetables to suit the individual palate. Pack tightly. Brush with marinade or barbecue sauce from time to time. The cooking time is usually about 10 minutes, or until the meat is nicely browned and tender. Push from the spears onto plates garnished with greens. Serve with a casserole of fluffy rice pilau and baskets heaped with French bread.

Wipe the skewers and proceed with the grilled-fruit dessert course.

Shish Kebab

2 pounds of lean lamb
8 tomatoes
16 mushroom caps

Marinade:
1 cup red wine
½ cup oil
2 tablespoons chopped onion
⅛ teaspoon pepper
1 mashed clove of garlic

Beforehand Preparation: Have the lamb cut in 1½-inch cubes. Mix the wine, oil, onion, pepper, and garlic and pour over the meat. Marinate for 8 hours. Slice tomatoes and quarter each slice.

At the Grill: Artistically arrange the lamb and vegetables on a large platter. Alternate lamb, mushrooms, tomatoes, and end with the third cube of lamb. Broil approximately 8 minutes, turning and basting to brown on all sides. Remove from skewers to hot plates and spoon a little marinade over all. Serves 4.

TRAY BOY: *lamb cubes, marinade, tomatoes, mushroom caps*

Menu

shish kebab
garlic French bread *
tossed green salad *
tangerines and cookies
coffee

Shashlik

a 6-pound leg of lamb
3 large onions
1 clove garlic
1 tablespoon salt
1 teaspoon black pepper
½ teaspoon powdered bay leaf
¼ teaspoon powdered rosemary
¼ teaspoon powdered ginger

Marinade:
1 cup oil
2 cups red wine vinegar

Beforehand Preparation: Bone the lamb. Cut into 7 or 8 1½-inch strips. Cut these into cubes. Sprinkle with a mixture of salt, pepper, bay leaf, rosemary, and ginger. Mash the garlic, chop the onion until fine. Place the meat in a bowl; work the onion, garlic, and meat together with your hands until the onion is well bruised. Pour the oil and wine vinegar over all and let marinate overnight in the refrigerator. Keep at room temperature for several hours before cooking.

At the Grill: Place the onion-clad meat on skewers or on a hand grill. Broil for about 5 minutes on each side close to the coals. Save the marinade, add more oil, and use on the tossed green salad.

TRAY BOY: *lamb cubes, marinade*

Menu

shashlik
julienne potatoes
hot rolls
tossed green salad
camembert cheese and crackers
red wine

Cocktail Kebabs

pitted olives wrapped in bacon
cocktail sausages
shrimp dipped in olive oil
squares of ham or luncheon
    meat
tiny tomatoes
pickled onions
chicken livers
cubes of cheese or pineapple
    wrapped in bacon

Alternate a combination of two or more of the above on small skewers and place over the grill. Turn until lightly brown on all sides. Serve as an hors d'oeuvre before the main feast, one skewerful for each guest. Provide napkins to protect their fingers from hot skewers.

Steak-and-Mushroom Kebab

1½ pounds round steak
½ pound of mushroom caps

Sauce:
1 teaspoon Worcestershire
    sauce
½ teaspoon MSG
1 clove garlic
⅛ teaspoon rosemary
½ cup red wine
½ cup oil
1 tablespoon horseradish

Beforehand Preparation: Cut the steak into 1½-inch squares. Wipe mushrooms with a damp cloth. Remove the stems and save for another dish. Marinate the steak and mushrooms in sauce for several hours.

At the Grill: Arrange steak cubes and mushrooms alternately on skewers or green sticks. Allow 3 cubes of steak and 2 mushrooms per skewer. Broil over bed of hot coals, basting frequently with sauce. Serve with remaining sauce. Serves 4.

TRAY BOY: *steak cubes, mushrooms, sauce*

Menu

steak-and-mushroom kebab
scalloped potatoes with onions
French bread *
broiled tomatoes *
fruit and cheese
coffee and brandy

Teriyakis

1 pound tender top round or sirloin ¾-inch thick
1 #2 can pineapple chunks
1 small jar stuffed olives

Marinade:
½ cup pineapple syrup
¼ cup soya sauce
1 clove garlic, chopped fine
¾ teaspoon ground ginger

Cut meat into bite-size cubes about the same size as the pineapple chunks. Combine pineapple syrup, soya sauce, garlic, and ginger; pour over the meat cubes and set aside at room temperature for 2 hours. Alternate cubes of meat and pineapple chunks on short skewers, finishing off with a stuffed olive. Broil, turning several times until a rich brown (10 to 12 minutes). Served snackwise, this will feed 8 people.

Incidentally, lamb or veal may be substituted for beef. Teriyakis are excellent to serve with rice and a salad for luncheon or supper. In that case, the meat may be cut in larger cubes, or longer skewers may be used. Serves 4 when used in this manner.

Steak-Bac-Pickebabs

8 slices top round beef ½-inch thick
8 dill pickles, medium-size
8 slices bacon

Spiral strips of steak around pickles and slices of bacon over steak strips. Fasten with small skewers. Impale on long skewers and grill until bacon is crisp on all sides. Serve on toasted frankfurter rolls. Serves 4.

Frankfurter-and-Cheese Kebabs

8 frankfurters
1 jar gherkins
4 tomatoes

½ pound cheddar cheese
¼ pound bacon

Cut the frankfurters in 1½-inch lengths. Cut each tomato into eight wedges. Cut the cheese into 1½-inch squares and wrap with bacon. Secure with toothpicks. Alternate on skewers, using two of everything with an extra frank for the end. Broil until the bacon is crisp, turning frequently. Serves 4.

Hawaiian Shrimp Kebab

2 pounds of jumbo shrimp
1 large can of pineapple
   chunks

½ pound bacon
½ cup soya sauce
2 lemons

Peel, de-vein shrimps. Pour the soya sauce over and stir occasionally for 15 minutes. Wrap the pineapple wedges in bacon. Secure with toothpicks broken in half. Alternate shrimps and pineapple on skewers and broil until the bacon is crisp. Serve with lemon wedges. Serves 4.

Ham and Pineapple on Skewers

1 pound prepared ham cut in 1½-inch cubes
1 large can pineapple chunks and juice

Spear cubes of ham and pineapple, allowing 3 cubes of ham and 2 of pineapple to each skewer. Broil for eight minutes, turning frequently, basting with pineapple juice. Serves 4.

Chicken Livers and Mushrooms en Brochette

12 chicken livers
½ pound bacon
½ pound mushroom caps

Cut the chicken livers in half. Wipe mushroom caps with a damp cloth. Remove mushroom stems and save for soup or sauce. Cut the bacon into 1-inch squares. Alternate chicken livers and mushroom caps, placing a square of bacon between each. Broil until bacon is done. Serves 4.

Calf's liver may be used instead of chicken livers. Water chestnuts may take the place of mushrooms in either case, and salami, the place of bacon.

Fish Kebab

2 pounds of fresh fish
2 cucumbers
½ pound bacon †

Sauce:
½ cup vinegar
1 bay leaf
6 crushed peppercorns
1 teaspoon salt
4 tablespoons oil

Beforehand Preparation: Marinate fish in sauce for several hours. Cut into 1-inch squares. Cut the cucumbers into discs ½-inch thick. Cut the bacon into 1-inch squares.

At the Grill: Spear the pieces on a skewer alternating one of each for 6 inches. Roast over the coals about 8 minutes, turning and basting often.

TRAY BOY: *fish, cucumbers, bacon, sauce*

Menu

stuffed-egg platter *
fish kebab
tossed-greens-and-avocado salad
corn sticks
banana nut roll *
tea

† If you prefer, substitute chunks of tomato for bacon.

Sweetbreads and Mushrooms en Brochette

2 pairs sweetbreads
1 tablespoon vinegar
5 strips bacon
½ pound mushroom caps

¼ cup melted butter or
  margarine
buttered bread crumbs

Beforehand Preparation: Soak the sweetbreads in cold water for an hour. Drain. Put in fresh water. Add vinegar and bring to a boil. Simmer 15 minutes. Reserve the rich stock for some future use. Plunge into cold water. When cool enough remove skin, membrane, and hard sinews. Cut them into 1½-inch cubes. Cut the bacon in 1½-inch squares.

At the Grill: Brush the mushrooms and sweetbreads with melted butter or margarine. Alternate sweetbreads, mushrooms, and bacon on the skewers. Grill for five minutes. Brush with melted butter and sprinkle with bread crumbs. Return to the grill, turning often until brown. Serves 4.

TRAY BOY: *sweetbreads, bacon, mushrooms, melted butter or margarine, bread crumbs*

Menu

sweetbreads and mushrooms en brochette
sweet gherkins, olives, celery
toasted cheese rolls
avocado-and-orange salad
sauterne

HAMBURGERS AND FRANKFURTERS

And Other Good Outdoor Specialties

What Makes Hamburgers Go to Heaven . . .

You do! The meat you buy, the preparation, and the cooking are the factors that make heavenly 'burgers. The choicest hamburgers are born at your meat market. Don't take run-of-the-shop meat. Insist on freshly ground bottom or top round. Watch what your butcher puts into the grinder. Ask him to eliminate most of the fat and put the meat through twice. Buy it as near cooking time as possible.

Lift lightly with a fork when combining the ingredients. Pat, don't crush, when shaping into cakes.

Don't over-season. Don't have too damp. Don't over-cook. Remember the chopped meat cooks quickly. Shape to fit buns.

Lemon juice or grated rind of lemon added to hamburger imparts tasty piquancy.

Add a minced clove of garlic to the grease or butter that the patties are to be fried in; discard garlic before cooking meat.

Brush the meat with soya sauce for a crispy brown exterior, pleasantly salt-flavored.

Sprinkle with Charcrust for a smoky flavor and crusty, charred exterior.

Pan-broiling saves the juices. At the last minute stir in a little water or wine and spoon over meat.

Have on hand spreads of relishes, pickles, mustard, and chili sauce.

Hamburgers for a Hungry Crowd

8 pounds of ground beef flank
4 tablespoons Worcestershire sauce
2 tablespoons seasoned salt
1 teaspoon freshly ground pepper

1 cup cracker meal
½ cup finely minced onions
3 beaten eggs
1 bowl bacon fat

Beforehand Preparation: Mix the seasonings. Sprinkle them over the meat, add cracker meal, onions, and eggs. Mix lightly until well-blended. Form into ¾-inch-thick patties. Arrange on a large tray in layers separated by wax paper. Make special chili sauce (your preference of recipes #1, 2, and 3).

At the Grill: Grease a large griddle and broil patties on each side until medium (about 5 to 7 minutes). Better not take special orders. Place between heated rolls. Let the guests help themselves to chili sauce.

TRAY BOY: *hamburger patties, bacon fat and brush, chili sauce*

Menu

hamburgers and rolls
chili sauce *
platter of bite-size raw vegetables *
watermelon boat *
lemonade or iced tea

Charcrust Hamburgers

2 slices white bread
¼ cup white wine
2 pounds ground top round
   steak
⅛ cup cold water

2 tablespoons grated onion
1 tablespoon tomato sauce
½ clove of crushed garlic
1 egg
½ teaspoon Charcrust

Beforehand Preparation: Trim crust off bread and soak slices in white wine. Squeeze excess wine out of bread. Then blend bread with all ingredients except Charcrust lightly but thoroughly with fork. After blending well, form mixture into good-sized cakes about 1½-inches thick.

At the Grill: Sprinkle Charcrust on meat. Place the patties on the grill and broil until crisply brown on both sides and interior reaches proper state of pinkness. Serve on buttered toasted rolls. Serves 6.

TRAY BOY: *meat patties, Charcrust*

Menu

Charcrust hamburgers on rolls
pick-and-choose salad *
devil's-food cake
iced tea

Hamburgers with Cheese Caps

1 pound bottom round, ground
    to order
6 slices cheddar cheese
3 tablespoons fat
3 large dill pickles
6 buns

1 teaspoon salt
1 teaspoon onion salt
¼ teaspoon freshly ground
    pepper
1 teaspoon Worcestershire
    sauce

Mix the meat and seasonings; form into 6 cakes about 1-inch thick. Cut pickles in slices. Heat an oblong griddle and grease. Brown the cakes and turn. Place a slice of cheese on the browned side. Cook about 5 minutes longer, or until meat is done as desired. Serve on toasted buns with pickle slices. Serves 6.

Hamburgers on a Hickory Stick

Here's a lot of fun for the 'teen agers at a picnic or barbecue.

1 pound ground hamburger
    meat
2 tablespoons bacon fat
1 teaspoon seasoned salt

2 tablespoons breadcrumbs
½ teaspoon poultry seasoning
1 egg
prepared hickory or green-
    wood spears

Combine all the ingredients. Wrap the meat in slender potato shapes around the sharpened end of each stick. Grill, turning slowly to brown all around. Place on hot frankfurter rolls. Serve chili sauce, India relish, and mustard on the side. For 4 hungry souls.

Hamburgers in Bacon Skirts

2 pounds lean beef
¼ cup heavy cream or
  condensed milk
2 tablespoons grated onion
1 teaspoon Worcestershire
  sauce
1 egg, beaten

½ teaspoon thyme
½ teaspoon marjoram
¼ teaspoon pepper
12 strips bacon
2 tablespoons soya sauce
6 hamburger buns

Beforehand Preparation: Form the meat, cream, onion, Worcestershire sauce, egg, pepper, and herbs into 5-inch patties. Bind them with bacon (2 strips each) and secure bacon with toothpicks. Sprinkle with soya sauce. Make special chili sauce, your choice of #1, 2, or 3.*

At the Grill: Place the hamburgers in a hand grill. Sear the 'burgers on each side and cook until done—about 5 to 7 minutes. Serve on toasted buns with chili sauce. Serves 6.

TRAY BOY: *hamburgers, chili sauce, toasted buns*

Menu

hamburgers in bacon skirts on toasted buns
garden salad bowl
melon filled with raspberries
beer or coffee

Hamburgers with Eggplant

1½ pounds choice ground beef
1 egg, beaten
1 tablespoon beer
1 teaspoon prepared mustard
1 minced medium onion
1 teaspoon Savor Salt

¼ teaspoon freshly ground
    pepper
1 large eggplant
seasoned flour
3 tablespoons butter

Beforehand Preparation: Pare and slice the eggplant in 4- by ¼-inch slices. Place in a bowl of salted water. Mix meat, egg, beer, mustard, onion, salt, and pepper. Form into patties the size of eggplant slices.

At the Grill: Wipe the eggplant slices and roll in seasoned flour. Sauté on buttered grill until brown. Remove and keep warm. Grill the hamburger patties. Place a slice of eggplant on a heated plate, a hamburger patty, then another slice of eggplant. Top with spicy barbecue or chili sauce. Serves 6.

TRAY BOY: *eggplant, seasoned flour, butter, hamburger patties*

Menu

hamburgers with eggplant
hashed-in-cream potatoes
Caesar salad *
nut-and-date loaf with whipped cream
coffee

Sweet-and-Sour Hamburgers

Grill the hamburgers. Place on buttered toast. Top with a slice of raw Bermuda onion and cover lightly with sugar.

Wienerburgers

2 pounds of chopped beef
1 tablespoon grated onion
2 tablespoons heavy cream
1 teaspoon Worcestershire
   sauce

1 teaspoon salt
1/4 teaspoon freshly ground
   pepper

Mix all the ingredients. Shape into long wiener-shaped "cigars." Grill and serve on hot, buttery toasted hot-dog rolls, with relishes galore. Serves 8.

Hollywood Hamburgers

1 pound ground beef
1 teaspoon salt
1/4 teaspoon freshly ground
   pepper
1/2 teaspoon poultry seasoning
2 tablespoons grated onion
butter

Relishes:
tomato slices
dill-pickle slices
onion slices
cheese slices
shredded lettuce
piccalilli

Lightly mix meat, seasoning and onion. Shape into thin 4-inch patties. Arrange the relishes on a large platter with piccalilli in a bowl on the side. Grill hamburgers in hand grill over hot coals. Butter heated rolls or buns (spread with mayonnaise if preferred). Pop in hamburger and top with any or all (!) of the relishes. Have plenty of napkins on hand. Serves 4.

Surprise Hamburgers

When you shape the patties hide an anchovy, olive, or small gherkin in the center.

Hamburger Tarts

Shape the meat into very thin cakes. On one cake place your choice of: a layer of thin cheese; a tablespoon of India relish; a tablespoon of bread stuffing; a tablespoon of minced onion and parsley; or a tablespoon of sautéed sliced mushrooms. Take it from there. You can think of a dozen variations to make taste buds tingle.

Beerburgers

2 pounds ground beef
salt and pepper
1 tablespoon grated onion
2 tablespoons fat
French bread

Sauce:
½ cup beer
½ cup catsup
2 tablespoons vinegar
2 tablespoons sugar
2 tablespoons Worcestershire
    sauce
salt and pepper to taste

Beforehand Preparation: Mix the meat with onion, salt and pepper to taste. Shape into 6 big, thick cakes. Combine all the ingredients for the sauce and mix well. Slice a long loaf of French bread, thinly at an angle. Butter on one side.

At the Grill: Brown the hamburger patties on both sides in sizzling hot fat, using a heavy skillet. Pour on sauce, simmer for 10 minutes. Meanwhile toast buttered bread slightly. Place 'burgers on bread and cover with sauce. Serves 6.

TRAY BOY: *hamburgers, fat, sauce, French bread*

Menu

beerburgers
macaroni doodad salad *
grapes and nuts
beer

Potatoburgers

1 pound hamburger	1 tablespoon A-1 Sauce
¼ cup minced onion	1 teaspoon salt
2 cups cooked potatoes, finely diced	⅛ teaspoon pepper
	fat

Mix hamburger, onion, potatoes, A-1 Sauce, salt and pepper. Shape into 6 thick patties. Grill on a hot greased griddle until golden brown on both sides. Serve on thin buttered toast with sliced tomatoes sprinkled with chives. Serves 6.

Frankfurter Suggestions

There are a thousand ways to cook the humble frank, and it is the tastiest morsel imaginable in the open air. Witness the tremendous sale of franks at the beaches and football games.

Cook them in boiling water for 2 minutes before roasting, grilling, etc.

1. They can be roasted on a flat griddle or on the end of a fork.

2. Cook them in barbecue sauce for a few minutes. Some frankfurters are packaged with a sealed bag of barbecue sauce in the can.

3. Slice them thin and add to scrambled eggs.

4. They make a whole meal out of one dish when added to black bean, split pea, or lentil soup. Heat the soup on your outdoor grill, chop in the little red discs of frankfurters, and serve with loads of crisp crackers and fruit for dessert.

5. Chop them into chef's or potato salad.

Franks à la Barbecue

12 frankfurters
¼ cup onion
¼ cup green pepper
3 tablespoons fat
1 scant teaspoon sugar

3 ripe tomatoes
¼ teaspoon basil
dash of Tabasco sauce
salt and pepper

Beforehand Preparation: Chop onions and pepper. Dip tomatoes in boiling water, slip off skins, and mash.

At the Grill: Melt fat in skillet and cook onion and pepper until soft. Add sugar, tomato, basil, Tabasco sauce, salt, and pepper to taste and simmer about 15 minutes. Cut franks in two lengthwise and put in a well-greased wire broiler. Broil, allowing about 3 minutes to each side. Serve covered with sauce. Serves 6.

TRAY BOY: *frankfurters, chopped pepper and onion, tomatoes, fat, sugar, salt, pepper mill, basil, Tabasco sauce*

Menu

potato chips with guacamole *
broiled frankfurters with barbecue sauce
baked beans *
Boston-brown-bread-and-butter sandwiches
fruit salad
iced tea

SERVICE NOTE: *When cooking this for youngsters use little if any pepper, Tabasco sauce or basil.*

Hot Dogs in Togs

8 frankfurters
mustard
pickle relish

8 pieces of bacon
toothpicks
rolls

Beforehand Preparation: Arrange the frankfurters and rolls on platters.

At the Grill: Split the frankfurters along the inside curve. Spread inside with a generous amount of prepared mustard or pickle relish. Wrap a piece of bacon spirally around the frank and secure with toothpicks. Impale on a skewer and roast over the grill until bacon is done. Serve on hot rolls. Serves 4.

TRAY BOY: *frankfurters, mustard, pickle relish, bacon, toothpicks, rolls*

Menu

hot dogs in togs on hot rolls
garden salad
baked bananas with lime juice *
coffee

Twisters

Mix a heavy biscuit dough; roll into long, thin pieces. Dip the end of a green stick in flour, wind the dough around it in a spiral, and bake over fire. To make them light, hold them close to the fire, turn slowly until the dough rises and a crust forms, then bake at a greater distance until a toothpick comes out dry.

Pigs in Blankets

Put a wiener on a sharpened stick and brown. While still hot, cover it with thick biscuit dough, just as with the Twisters.

Char-Franks

Pre-cook the frankfurters until tender. Cut in halves and sprinkle the flat side with Charcrust. Place over grill with flat side down for one minute. Taste before adding any additional condiment.

Cajun Frankfurters

6 frankfurters	½ cup catsup
1 chopped medium onion	2 tablespoons dark brown
1 chopped green pepper	sugar
⅓ cup sweet-pickle relish	2 teaspoons prepared mustard
⅓ cup vinegar	¼ teaspoon Tabasco sauce

Combine all ingredients, except frankfurters, in a saucepan. Bring to boiling point; reduce heat and simmer 10 minutes. Place frankfurters in barbecue sauce and simmer 20 minutes longer. Serves 6.

Frankfurters and Sauerkraut in a Skillet

8 frankfurters	¼ teaspoon caraway seeds
2½ cups juicy sauerkraut	2 tablespoons brown sugar
2 tablespoons butter	2 green apples

Beforehand Preparation: Core and halve apples.

At the Grill: Melt the butter in a skillet. Sauté the apples until brown. Remove and keep warm. Place the sauerkraut in skillet and sprinkle with caraway seeds. Make a hollow down length of center, line frankfurters down center. Put apples cut side up on sauerkraut near the edge of skillet. Sprinkle the apples with brown sugar. Cover and simmer 15 minutes. Serves 4.

TRAY BOY: *butter, apples, sauerkraut, caraway seeds, frankfurters, sugar*

Menu

frankfurters, sauerkraut, and apples
spoon bread
banana-cream pie
beer

Grilled Bacon Sandwiches

8 rolls   pepper
16 strips of thick bacon   ¼ lb. of butter
8 slices of tomato

Beforehand Preparation: Check the pepper mill to see that it is filled with pepper corns, and arrange the rolls, bacon and tomato slices on separate platters.

At the Grill: The bacon can be broiled over your grill surface if the stripping is fine enough. Or you may use a flat griddle or skillet. While the bacon is becoming crisp and brown, slice the rolls and brown them, cut side down, on a hot griddle which has been generously buttered. Put a slice of tomato on each roll, sprinkle with pepper, and top with 4 half strips of bacon. You'll have plenty of reorders for this dish. Serves 4.

TRAY BOY: *rolls, bacon, tomato slices, pepper mill, butter*

Menu

grilled-bacon sandwiches
potato salad *
a dish of assorted pickles and relishes
baked apples on a stick

3. Fish & Shellfish

Fish, a festival food in practically all countries of the World, may justly be called one of the sportsman's and outdoor chef's favorite dishes. It is versatile to handle and prepare, may be pan fried, grilled over the coals, or "en papillote" with admirable results. And don't forget fish has plenty of vitamins, is non-fattening, tastes good and is good for your budget.

FISH AND SHELLFISH

Marine Delicacies Make a Feast of Fasting

Poissons en Papillote
à la James T. Brown of Hawaii

2 large trout	pepper
2 buds crushed garlic	good pinch marjoram
salt	good pinch thyme

Beforehand Preparation: Purchase or catch your fish and have it cleaned and gutted. Some people prefer having heads and tails cut off. Get some good brown wrapping paper from your butcher or grocer, or better yet, some parchment paper. Have it about 2½ inches wider than the fish on either end and long enough so that you can fold the fish in it three to four times. Now oil or grease the paper on both sides. Put marjoram and thyme in the fishes' bellies and rub in mashed garlic. Salt and pepper the outside of the fish. Place on greased paper, roll over once, fold ends under, and finish rolling. Tie in middle with greased string.

At the Grill: This can be cooked in the oven, under the broiler, or in a spider over some not too hot coals on the barbecue. Should the paper start to scorch, brush with the grease. Turn every 10 minutes for about 30 minutes. Unwrap and slide off onto your plate. There you'll have a dish of fish such as you have never tasted before. All of the fish flavor, no grease, and no odor. Some people have asked me to put in chopped onions, chopped celery, and chopped mushrooms—and lemon juice! Who would think of insulting a nice fresh fish with lemon juice? The use of lemon juice came from the old days in Germany before the fast fish trains went into service, and some of the fish got rather high. The lemon juice was used to do away with that odor. Serves 6 to 8.

TRAY BOY: *trout en papillote, fat*

Menu

poissons en papillote à la Brown
green peas cooked with minced onion and garnished with mint
French-fried potatoes
sautéed eggplant *
watermelon
iced tea

Stuffed Fresh Haddock

a haddock of about 3 pounds
dash of garlic salt
salt and pepper
flour
1 tablespoon melted margarine
fat

Stuffing:
1 cooked onion
3 tablespoons breadcrumbs
1 tablespoon butter
½ teaspoon salt
⅛ teaspoon pepper
1 tablespoon chopped parsley
1 beaten egg

Beforehand Preparation: Chop the onion and mix breadcrumbs, melted butter, salt, pepper, chopped parsley and egg. Rub the fish inside and out with a mixture of salt, pepper and garlic salt. Stuff and sew the fish.

At the Grill: Brush the fish with melted margarine. Dredge with flour. Grease both sides of a piece of brown paper cut 2½ inches wider than the length of fish and long enough to fold the fish 4 times. Fold the fish into the paper, turning end flaps under after the first roll. Tie with greased string. Cook in outdoor oven or on the grill over low coals. Turn 3 times during the 30 minutes it takes to cook. Keep the paper from scorching by brushing with grease.

TRAY BOY: *stuffed fish, margarine, flour, paper, fat, string*

Menu

chilled tomato juice
stuffed fresh haddock
shredded cucumbers with **sour-cream sauce** *
hot potato chips
French rolls
fresh fruit and cheese
café espresso

Grill-Baked Stuffed Fish

a large fish weighing 5 to 7
  pounds
  (trout, salmon, red snapper,
  shad, bass, or haddock)
3/4 cup each chopped green
  pepper, celery, and onions
1/4 cup of minced parsley
1 cup of water mixed with 1/4
  cup of oil

1 teaspoon of salt
pinch of thyme
pinch of marjoram
1/2 teaspoon of pepper
parsley for garnish
3 tablespoons of butter
1 teaspoon of lemon juice

Beforehand Preparation: Remove the head, clean and rinse fish. Wipe inside and out with salt and lemon. Stuff with the chopped vegetables, herbs, salt, and pepper (or use a bread dressing). Sew the body securely.

At the Grill: Place the fish on a piece of chicken wire cut to size. Fold the wire into a form-fitting basket and fasten the loose ends into the mesh. Arrange on the grill and cook for 1½ hours, turning and basting with the water-oil mixture. Remove the wire and place the fish on a heated platter or plank. Remove any remaining pieces of skin which may have been left on the fish. Most of it will come off with the wire. Blend melted butter and lemon juice. Garnish with parsley and serve with lemon butter. Serves 8-10.

TRAY BOY: *stuffed fish, parsley, lemon, butter, water, oil*

Menu

  grill-baked stuffed fish
  lemon butter
  frenched string beans
  scalloped potatoes
  Chinese ginger preserves with cream cheese
  tea with lemon and cloves

Bass and Bacon †

    4 double fish fillets
    pepper
    16 slices of bacon

   Beforehand Preparation: Skin and bone the fish fillets, leaving the two sides joined. Flatten the double fish fillets.

   At the Grill: Season with pepper. Lay each double fillet over 2 pieces of criss-crossed bacon on a double sided wire grill. Criss-cross two more pieces on the top side of each fish and close the grill. Cook 6 inches from the coals, turning frequently until the bacon is crisp. Serve at once. Serves 4.

   Tray boy: *4 double fish fillets, pepper, bacon*

Menu

    bass and bacon
    country-fried potatoes
    cole-slaw sprinkled with celery seed *
    cornbread sticks
    cherry tarts
    campfire coffee

   † You can prepare trout, sunfish, perch, etc., in the same manner.

Pan-Fried Fish Manitowish †

4 strips of bacon
a freshly caught fish
salt
pepper

flour
corn meal
lemon slices

Beforehand Preparation: Clean the fish and divide into two fillets.

At the Grill: Fry the bacon in a cast-iron skillet. Remove to brown paper and keep warm. Rub the fish inside and out with salt, pepper, and flour mixed with corn meal. Place the fillets in the hot fat, skin side down. Work the skillet back and forth so that the hot fat cooks the fish over and under. Brown on both sides. Drain on brown paper and serve hot with lemon slices and crispy bacon. On a camping trip, this is a treat from the gods of nature that you can serve for breakfast, luncheon, or dinner. Serves 2.

TRAY BOY: *bacon, fish, salt, pepper, flour, corn meal, lemon slices*

Menu

pan-fried fish
new potatoes in their jackets
buttered peas
skillet bread
Gruyère cheese and crackers
campfire coffee

† Manitowish was a great Indian chief whose descendants now guide fishermen through the bountiful lakes of Wisconsin. Nothing tastes better than to cook your own catch by the lakeside while listening to the wondrous Indian lore of these guides.

Steamed Fish

a freshly caught fish weighing
    1 pound or more
salt
pepper

fat
paper
lemon
butter

Beforehand Preparation: Clean the fish and rub with salt and pepper. Prepare lemon butter.

At the Grill: Grease a sheet of brown paper thoroughly on both sides. Place the fish on the paper and roll. Secure so that the fish is closely encased. Dip a newspaper in water and roll around the bundle until there are about 12 thicknesses. Place this in a cavity in the middle of a bed of coals and cover with coals. A 1-pound fish will take about 20 minutes. Allow 10 additional minutes for each extra pound. Figure on ½ pound per person. When you remove the paper, the skin will come off with it, leaving just the succulent meat, which has stewed in its own juice. Serve with lemon butter and freshly ground pepper. Serves 2.

TRAY BOY: *fish, fat, paper, lemon butter*

Menu

steamed fish
baked potatoes
sliced tomatoes sprinkled with basil
blueberry muffins
fresh peaches and cream
coffee

Fish Fillet Flipflop

6 good-sized fish fillets
olive oil or butter
flour as needed

salt and pepper to taste
barbecue sauce

Beforehand Preparation: Half an hour before needed, place fish fillets on sheet of waxed paper. Brush with olive oil; dredge with flour.

At the Grill: Have ready two cookie sheets. Grease with butter or oil. Place fillets on one sheet. Place sheet over fire. Cook 4 minutes. Take from fire and place second sheet over first, greased side up. Hold sheets together and turn very quickly, and the uncooked sides of the fillets will be on bottom. Broil as before. When done, slide onto warmed serving platter. Season fillets and pour any favorite sauce over them. Garnish with parsley. Serves 6.

TRAY BOY: *floured fish fillets, butter or oil as needed, 2 cookie sheets, salt, pepper mill, sauce*

Menu

clam-and-tomato broth
fish fillets with sauce
brown-bread-and-cucumber sandwiches *
small potatoes in parsley butter
beets with sour sauce
endive salad
toasted crackers and cheese
choice of beverage

SERVICE NOTE: *This is an excellent way of cooking thin fillets, eliminating the usual difficulty in turning. Skill is developed with practice.*

Broiled Lobster

4 live lobsters
salt
freshly ground pepper
½ cup melted butter

Tabasco sauce
watercress
garlic salt
lemon wedges

Beforehand Preparation: Wash lobsters, then split by inserting heavy knife between eyes and cutting toward tail on stomach side. Insert knife very quickly between the eyes and into brain so as to kill the lobster instantly. When splitting, be careful not to go through back shell. Clean out intestinal tract and stomach. Crack claws lightly with small hammer. Brush with melted butter or margarine; sprinkle with a little salt and grind on plenty of fresh pepper.

At the Grill: Broil on the back side until the shell is browned and the meat tender. It usually takes 15 minutes, but depends on size of lobster and distance from heat. Baste every 4 or 5 minutes with melted butter. Season and serve on large heated plates garnished with watercress and lemon wedges. Serve with little containers of hot melted butter seasoned with a dash or two of Tabasco sauce and a sprinkle of garlic salt. Serves 4.

TRAY BOY: *prepared lobsters, cup of melted butter and brush, seasoned salt, pepper grinder, watercress, Tabasco sauce, garlic salt*

Menu

broiled lobsters
hot potato chips
lettuce, apple, and avocado salad
hot finger rolls
chilled melon
beer or white wine

"French Quarter" Shrimps in Barbecue Sauce

3 pounds of shrimp
1 teaspoon salt
1 stalk celery
1 bay leaf

Sauce:
¼ cup oil
1 bunch sliced scallions with green tops
¼ cup chopped celery
¼ cup chopped green pepper

1 #2 can tomatoes
1 bay leaf
1 clove mashed garlic
1 teaspoon Worcestershire sauce
¼ teaspoon thyme
¼ teaspoon ground clove
¼ cup lemon juice
3 thin slices of lemon peel
1 teaspoon salt
1 cup sherry wine

Beforehand Preparation: Clean shrimps as usual, removing shell and black vein in back. Boil them for 15 minutes in 1½ quarts of water with 1 teaspoon salt, a stalk of celery, and 1 bay leaf.

At the Grill: Heat the oil in a large skillet. Cook the scallions, green pepper and celery until they soften. Add tomatoes, bay leaf, and garlic. Simmer for 5 minutes and add all the other ingredients, except the shrimp and half of the wine. Simmer for 15 minutes, then add the cooked shrimp and the remaining wine. Cook until the shrimp is heated through and serve at once. Serves 8.

TRAY BOY: *oil, scallions, celery, green pepper, tomatoes, bay leaf, garlic, Worcestershire sauce, thyme and clove, lemon juice and peel, salt, wine, shrimps*

Menu

guacamole * and Tortillas
"French Quarter" shrimp
fluffy white rice *
hot biscuits and butter
minted strawberries and cream
beverage

Soya Shrimp †

3 pounds of large shrimp
½ cup soya sauce
½ cup melted margarine

¼ cup lemon juice
chopped parsley

Beforehand Preparation: Peel and clean shrimp. Chop parsley. Melt margarine and mix with lemon juice.

At the Grill: Marinate the shrimps in soya sauce for 5 minutes, turning several times. String them close together on several skewers and place across the top of the grill about 9 inches from the coals. Baste several times with the margarine-and-lemon mixture. After 9 minutes turn and broil the other side for 3 minutes. Place on hot plates, pour remaining barbecue sauce over shrimps, and sprinkle with parsley. Serves 6.

TRAY BOY: *shrimp, soya sauce, margarine-and-lemon mixture, parsley*

Menu

soya shrimp
sizzling bananas *
young spinach salad
corn dodgers *
rhubarb pie
beer or coffee

† Crayfish, prawns, lobster tails, smelts, sardines, or porgies can be cooked in this manner.

Shrimps à la Barbecue

32 medium-sized canned or
    fresh-cooked shrimps
¼ cup butter
1 small minced onion
2 scant tablespoons flour

1 pint milk
¼ cup catsup
½ teaspoon chili powder
salt and pepper to taste
parsley

Beforehand Preparation: Rinse and dry cooked shrimps. Mince onion.

At the Grill: Melt butter in skillet and cook onion until soft. Sprinkle on the flour and blend in a little milk. Add more until you have used about a cup. Add catsup and other seasoning and more milk to make sauce of desired consistency. Add shrimps and cook 3 or 4 minutes. Serve on freshly boiled rice. Garnish with parsley. Serves 4.

TRAY BOY: *shrimps, butter, flour, milk, onion, catsup, chili powder, salt, pepper mill, parsley*

Menu

corn chowder
shrimps on rice
roasted corn *
roasted potatoes *
apple dumplings with hard sauce
tea

SERVICE NOTE: *If you are roasting corn and potatoes in hot ashes you should allow about an hour for potatoes and 10 to 12 minutes for corn.*

Jambalaya

3 cups cleaned cooked shrimps
3 slices diced bacon
1 clove mashed garlic
3 tablespoons chopped onion
3 tablespoons chopped celery
3 tablespoons chopped green
  pepper
2 tablespoons parsley
1 tablespoon flour
1 bay leaf

¼ teaspoon thyme
dash of Tabasco sauce
½ teaspoon chili powder
¼ teaspoon powdered clove
3 cups tomatoes
1½ cups rice
1 cup cooked mushrooms
1 small can chopped pimentos
salt to taste

Beforehand Preparation: Prepare the chopped vegetables, bacon, and shrimp.

At the Grill: Use a large skillet with cover or a Dutch oven for this. Try out bacon. Add garlic, onion, celery, pepper, and parsley. Cook until soft; blend in flour. Add bay leaf, thyme, Tabasco, chili powder, clove, and tomatoes. Cover and simmer for 30 minutes. Meanwhile cook the rice.* Break the shrimps in small pieces. Add shrimp, mushrooms, salt to taste, and pimento. Simmer for 5 minutes. Add cooked rice. Stir gently but thoroughly. Serve very hot. Serves 6.

TRAY BOY: *shrimps, diced bacon, onion, celery, garlic, green pepper, parsley, flour, bay leaf, thyme, Tabasco sauce, chili powder, clove, tomatoes, rice, mushrooms, pimentos, salt*

Menu

salted nuts
jambalaya
cucumber-and-onion sandwiches *
avocado-and-celery salad
strawberry whip on sponge cake *
coffee

Curried Prawns

2 dozen prawns
4 shallots
1 clove mashed garlic
½ green pepper
1 cup coconut milk
1 tablespoon curry powder
a dash of turmeric

½ teaspoon of cinnamon
½ teaspoon powdered cloves
2 slices lemon peel
1 teaspoon powdered bay leaf
1 teaspoon salt
juice of one lemon

Beforehand Preparation: Mince shallots and green pepper. Make coconut milk by softening the meat of a fresh coconut in hot water and squeezing it through a cloth. Cook prawns in boiling salted water for 10 minutes.

At the Grill: Lightly brown shallots, garlic, and green pepper in a heavy skillet. Add curry powder, turmeric, cinnamon, cloves, lemon peel and bay leaf. Blend for a few minutes into a paste. Add coconut milk and salt. Cook very slowly for 3 minutes. Add prawns, cook another 5 minutes, remove from the fire, discard lemon peel, add lemon juice, and serve with rice. Serves 6.

TRAY BOY: *shallots, garlic, green pepper, bay leaf, lemon juice and peel, curry powder, turmeric, cinnamon, cloves, coconut milk, salt, prawns, rice*

Menu

curried prawns
condiment tray:
   roasted coconut slices
   pickled mushrooms
   cottage cheese sprinkled with chives
   chutney
   chopped nuts
saffron rice *
chiffonade salad *
lime sherbet
beer or ale

Squantum Clam Fritters

3 dozen razor-neck or quahog
    clams
fat
butter
lemon wedges
parsley

Batter:
1¼ cups flour
2 teaspoons baking powder
⅛ teaspoon pepper
¼ teaspoon salt
⅓ cup clam liquid
⅓ cup milk

Beforehand Preparation: Mix all batter ingredients until smooth about 2 hours before using.

At the Grill: Shuck and clean clams, remove beard. Wipe dry. Heat 3 or 4 inches of fat in a heavy pot 'til a drop of water dances in it. Dip clams in batter and fry in hot fat until golden brown. Serve at once with butter sauce. Garnish with parsley and lemon wedges. Serves 6.

TRAY BOY: *clams, batter, fat, butter sauce, lemon wedges, parsley*

Menu

clam chowder *
Squantum clam fritters
roast corn on the cob *
cole slaw *
Indian pudding
coffee

Boat Steerers (clam fritters)

1 pint clams, drained and
    chopped
1 egg
⅔ cup milk

1¼ cups flour, sifted before
    measuring
2 teaspoons baking powder
¼ teaspoon salt

Beforehand Preparation: Prepare the clams and drain well after chopping.

At the Grill: Mix egg with milk. Sift flour with baking powder and salt. Combine with milk and mix to a smooth batter. Have fresh frying fat or oil in kettle and set over fire to heat. Now mix drained chopped clams thoroughly with batter, and when fat is about 370 degrees drop clam batter in large spoonfuls into hot fat. If fritter falls apart, you may have to add a little more flour to batter. Drain fritters on absorbent paper and serve as quickly as possible.

TRAY BOY: *chopped clams, flour, baking powder, salt, egg, milk, frying fat*

Menu

    olive-and-cream-cheese canapés
    clam fritters
    carrot balls
    peas
    chilled asparagus salad
    jam tarts
    beer or ale

SERVICE NOTE: *If you are not versed in the art of fritter-frying you should have at least one dress rehearsal for this turn. Be sure to use a fat thermometer.*

Grilled Oysters or Clams

24 oysters or 32 clams
butter
pepper

minced crisp bacon (optional)
chopped parsley
wedges of lemon

Beforehand Preparation: Scrub the shells clean. Rinse well. Prepare bacon if you plan to use it.

At the Grill: Leave the shellfish intact in their shells. Place them on the hot grill. When the shells pop open they are done. Place a piece of butter on each one and sprinkle with parsley and bacon. Pass the pepper grinder, squeeze on some lemon juice, and go to it. They are delicious. Serves 4.

TRAY BOY: *oysters, butter, pepper mill, parsley, bacon, lemon*

Menu

grilled oysters or clams
baked potatoes *
romaine-and-avocado salad with tart dressing
toasted poppy-seed rolls
fruit-and-cheese platter
beer

Shipwrecked Oysters

36 oysters on half shell
rock salt
½ cup catsup
¼ teaspoon Worcestershire
    sauce

½ cup grated American cheese
butter
2 lemons
parsley

Beforehand Preparation: You will need two roasting pans for 36 oysters. In bottom of each put a layer of rock salt about 1 inch deep. Arrange oysters on half shell on top of salt. Cut lemons into wedges.

At the Grill: Sprinkle catsup on each oyster, then a little Worcestershire sauce and grated cheese. Put a dab of butter on top and place pans in brisk oven for 5 or 6 minutes. Take from oven,† remove oysters, and spread hot rock salt on soup plates. Place 6 oysters on top of each plate and garnish with wedges of lemon and sprigs of parsley. Serves 6.

TRAY BOY: *oysters on rock salt, catsup, Worcestershire sauce, grated cheese, butter, lemon, parsley*

Menu

jellied consommé
shipwrecked oysters
hot corn bread
mixed vegetables in French dressing *
baked apples with whipped cream
iced coffee

† Excellent, too, cooked on top of grill.

Oysters in Blankets

24 oysters
Tabasco sauce
½ cup chopped parsley
24 thin slices of bacon
box of toothpicks
1 cup of catsup

3 tablespoons of horseradish
8 slices of day-old white bread
2 eggs
½ teaspoon of salt
⅔ cup milk
2 tablespoons margarine

Beforehand Preparation: Wash the oysters, running hands through to remove any pieces of shell. Mix the catsup and horseradish.

At the Grill: Sprinkle each oyster with a dash of Tabasco sauce and some chopped parsley. Roll a slice of bacon around it and secure with a toothpick. Impale on a skewer and broil over the hot coals until the bacon is crisp. In the meantime, beat the eggs slightly in a low pan. Add the salt and milk. Dip the slices of bread into the mixture. Place a griddle over the grill and heat the margarine until it sizzles. Brown the bread and keep it hot. Place the sizzling oysters on the French toast and top with the catsup-horseradish mixture. Serves 8.

TRAY BOY: *oysters, Tabasco sauce, parsley, slices of bacon, toothpicks, catsup-and-horseradish mixture, bread, eggs, salt, milk, margarine*

Menu

oysters in blankets on French toast
chilled garden salad with creamy dressing
seedless green grapes
cookies
coffee

Broiled Crumbed Oysters

24 oysters   1 cup cracker crumbs
½ cup butter   salt and pepper to taste

Beforehand Preparation: Scrub oysters thoroughly.

At the Grill: Place oysters in wire broiler or on grill until shells open. Remove from shells and place on paper towel with another towel on top to absorb juice. Dip each oyster in melted butter, sprinkle with salt and pepper, and then dip in crumbs. Place on well-greased wire broiler, turning 3 or 4 times while broiling. This will take 5 or 6 minutes. Serves 4.

> TRAY BOY: *oysters, butter, cracker crumbs, salt, pepper mill*

Menu

mushroom soup
broiled oysters
asparagus on toast with lemon wedges
cabbage salad *
fruit sherbet, little cakes
iced tea

SERVICE NOTE: *As a matter of convenience, use canned soups for outdoor cooking, "doctoring" them to suit your taste, if you like. Even the best amateur chefs do this.*

Fisherman's Mussels

1 quart mussels
4 medium onions
1 large can evaporated milk
2 tablespoons fine cracker
    crumbs
2 tablespoons butter

1 pinch mace
1 teaspoon salt
¼ teaspoon freshly ground
    pepper
paprika

Beforehand Preparation: Scrub the mussels carefully. Discard any with open shells. Steam them open in 1½ cups of water. When they open up they are done. Do not overcook. Remove them from their shells. Strain the liquor in which they have been cooking.

At the Grill: Slice the onions and place in the liquor. Add the cracker crumbs, mace, salt, and pepper. Bring to a boil. Heat the milk on the side. Add the mussels to the liquor and simmer gently for 1 minute. Dish the mussels with some of the broth into bowls. Add hot milk, a piece of butter, and a sprinkle of paprika. Serves 4.

TRAY BOY: *mussels and liquor, onions, milk, cracker crumbs, mace, salt, pepper, butter, paprika*

Menu

fisherman's mussels
pilot biscuits
tossed lettuce, watercress, and tomatoes with French dressing
compote of fruit
beer

Broiled Frogs' Legs

12 pairs of frogs' legs
6 slices of toast

Marinade:
¾ cup of oil
⅓ cup of lemon juice
salt
freshly ground pepper
1 clove of mashed garlic

Beforehand Preparation: Marinate the frogs' legs in oil, lemon juice, salt, pepper, and the mashed clove of garlic for 30 to 45 minutes before cooking. Turn them in the marinade three or four times.

At the Grill: Place them on a two-sided wire grill. Fasten grill and broil them over low coals, basting with the marinade every few minutes. Cook 5-6 minutes on each side or until done. Serve on crisp buttered toast. Serves 6.

TRAY BOY: *frogs' legs, marinade, toast*

Menu

broiled frogs' legs on toast
asparagus tips with butter sauce
molded Bing-cherry salad
chilled white wine or iced tea

Frog Fry

8 pairs of frogs' legs
salt
paprika
flour
3 tablespoons of butter

2 cloves of chopped garlic
¾ cup of Spanish
   mayonnaise *
1 lemon cut into 8 wedges

Beforehand Preparation: Skin the frogs' legs just as you would peel a glove from your hand. Wash them in cold water. Soak in salted water for 15 minutes and store them in the refrigerator. One hour before use take them out and keep at room temperature.

At the Grill: Dust the frogs' legs with salt and paprika; roll them in flour. In a large skillet heat the butter over medium coals. Sauté the chopped garlic in this for 4 minutes. Discard the garlic. Lay in the frogs' legs and fry to a rich brown. Drain on paper. Serve with Spanish mayonnaise and lemon wedges. Serves 4.

TRAY BOY: *frogs' legs, flour, salt, paprika, butter or other fat, garlic, Spanish mayonnaise, lemon wedges*

Menu

frogs' legs with Spanish mayonnaise * and lemon wedges
French-fried potato sticks
cucumber salad with French dressing
hot rolls
fruit
coffee

Norwich Clambake

rock seaweed
cheesecloth
16 small potatoes in scrubbed
    jackets
16 small onions
2 quartered broiling chickens

4 small lobsters, split and
    cleaned
8 sausages
8 ears of corn, a layer of husk
    left on
3 quarts of well-cleaned clams

Beforehand Preparation: Clean and prepare vegetables, chickens, lobsters, sausages and clams.

At the Grill: For a perfect clambake at home or the beach, you spread a thickness of seaweed on bottom of clam steamer, washtub or large kettle. Wrap each layer in cheesecloth and spread out flat. Arrange a cushion of seaweed between each layer. First layer: potatoes and onions. Second layer: chickens. Third layer: lobsters, sausages, and corn. Fourth layer: clams. Top with seaweed and one potato. (When potato is done, then everything else is cooked.) Cover and steam over a wood or charcoal fire for 1½ hours. The mixed juices and rockweed make 3 quarts of delicious broth, tinted slightly by the rockweed and flavored by chicken and sausage. Serve with large dishes of melted butter for each person. Serves 8.

TRAY BOY: *seaweed, cheesecloth, potatoes and onions, chickens, lobsters, sausages, corn, clams*

Menu

broth and clams
corn, sausages, and lobsters
chickens, potatoes, and onions
chunks of French bread
beer or coffee

Seafood Bake

Construct a fire on a large flat rock or rocks surrounded by a few protecting stones. When the fire dies down and rocks are extremely hot, cover with a mass of seaweed. Into the nest of seaweed place the crustaceans. You may have mussels, clams, lobster, or crabs. Corn on the cob, onions, and potatoes will bake deliciously. Give the potatoes a head start in the ashes of the fire. If you have a fish, wrap it well in greased brown paper and add it. Now take more seaweed and cover the food. Throw a piece of canvas or a burlap bag over all and let it steam for an hour. Then fall to. Here's a feast for the gods.

Notes About Steamed Clams

Last summer when we steamed clams, we quite often placed a few stalks of celery, a crushed clove of garlic, and a few fresh herbs on top. We found that it improved the flavor.

At shore bakes, hard- or soft-shelled clams, oysters, and mussels are favorites, the soft-shelled clam being easiest to prepare. Cherrystones have the sweetest meat. Allow about 15 or 20 clams per person.

Strain and drink the delightful nourishing broth first, then start on the clams, slipping off and discarding the hairy beard with the shells. Dip in a small dish of broth and then into butter and pop the clam into your mouth. Fingers are best for this. If you have some broth left, take it home to serve iced next day or to use as jellied clam broth.

Steamed Clams

4 quarts of clams   1 tablespoon mustard
1 cup of water   butter
½ cup of corn meal

Beforehand Preparation: Fill a bucket with water. Add corn meal and mustard. Put clams in water for six hours. They will practically clean themselves. Discard any broken or wide-open clams. Scrub off any remaining film with a brush, changing the water several times as you work.

At the Grill: Pack them tightly in bottom of steamer. Add about a cup of water. Cover closely and steam over a driftwood fire or a portable grill, and when the shells begin to open, the clams are done. Too much steaming makes clams tough. Melt butter and serve in individual dishes. Add lemon juice and/or Tabasco sauce if you like. Serve strained broth in side cups. Arrange clams on large plates or bowls. Serves 6.

TRAY BOY: *clams, butter*

Menu

    steamed clams
    melted butter
    broth
    tossed salad of greens and cucumbers
    hot rolls
    honeydew melon
    choice of beer or coffee

Down East Clam Chowder †

4 thin slices of salt pork
1 large chopped onion
4 cups of diced potatoes
3 tablespoons flour
1 teaspoon salt
freshly ground pepper
2 quarts of boiling clam juice
  and water

2 tablespoons of butter
1 quart of chopped clams or
  2 #1 cans of minced clams
1 quart of evaporated milk
parsley
pilot crackers

Beforehand Preparation: Examine the clams for pieces of shell and cut off the hard necks. Chop the necks very fine. Cut the bodies of the clams into quarters. Save the juice, straining it through cheesecloth.

At the Grill: Heat the Dutch oven and try out the slices of salt pork. Add the onion and cook until soft. Put the potatoes and the chopped necks in, sprinkle with flour, salt, and freshly ground pepper. Add the boiling liquid and simmer for 17 minutes. Add the milk and soft clams, return to the boiling point, and cook for 2 minutes. Top with 2 tablespoons of butter and a sprinkle of parsley. Pour the chowder over pilot crackers in soup plates and serve. Serves 12.

> TRAY BOY: *salt pork, onion, potatoes, flour, salt, and pepper, liquid from clams and water, butter, clams with soft and hard parts separated, milk, pilot crackers, parsley*

Menu

Down East clam chowder
pilot crackers
chef's salad *
watermelon
beer or coffee

† For Fish Chowder, substitute an equivalent amount of haddock, cod, halibut or red snapper for the clams.

Bouillabaisse

1 fresh haddock
1 lobster
24 clams and juice
12 scallops
½ pound of crabmeat lumps
2 tomatoes, cut in wedges
½ pound of minced onions
4 cloves of mashed garlic

2 bay leaves
1 pinch thyme
1 pinch saffron
1 chopped carrot
1 teaspoon olive oil
1 strip of orange or lemon peel
1 cup sauterne
chopped parsley

Beforehand Preparation: Wash and cut the vegetables. Clean and cut the fish and lobster to bite-size pieces.

At the Grill: Heat the oil and arrange the vegetables, herbs, and orange peel in the bottom of a cast-iron Dutch oven. Let them simmer for 7 minutes and then lay the fish on top of the vegetables, *not the clams.* Add 2 quarts of liquid—clam juice and water—and bring to a boil. Cook 18 minutes, add the clams, and cook 4 minutes longer. Add the sauterne and bring to a boil again. Serve at once. Place the solid food on hot plates and pour some of the broth over it. Sprinkle with parsley. Serves a crowd.

> TRAY BOY: *fish cut into pieces, tomatoes, onions, and carrots, oil, garlic, bay leaf, thyme, and saffron, citrus peel, sauterne, parsley*

Menu

bouillabaisse
toast pan-fried in butter
crisp tossed green salad
sauterne

Cioppino

The famous San Francisco Fisherman's Wharf version of bouillabaisse is a fish stew in tomato sauce. Wear a bib when you dip into this. You'll eat it with gusto.

½ cup olive oil
1 large crab
1 pound shrimp
1 pound clams with juice
2 pounds fish, such as barra-
    cuda, red snapper, sea bass,
    etc.
1 lobster
1 cup parsley

6 green onions and tops,
    chopped
2 cloves mashed garlic
1 bay leaf
salt
pepper
½ teaspoon basil
1 cup white wine
1 #2½ can tomatoes

Beforehand Preparation: Clean all fish and shellfish, leaving clams in their shells. Cut the fish, crab, and lobster in pieces. Chop the onions and parsley. Mash garlic.

At the Grill: Use a Dutch oven or a large, heavy pot. Heat the oil, add the onions, garlic, and parsley. Simmer covered for a few minutes. Add the tomatoes, bay leaf, and clam juice. Simmer for 20 minutes. Add all the fish except the clams. Add the basil and wine. Simmer for 15 minutes. Add the clams, season to taste with salt and pepper, simmer for 10 minutes, and serve. Serves 6.

TRAY BOY: *oil, crab, shrimp, fish, and lobster, clams and juice, onions, garlic, and parsley, tomatoes, bay leaves, basil, salt and pepper, wine*

Menu

cioppino
garlic French bread
chickory, escarole and romaine salad
peach cobbler
white wine

4. *Eggs*

Eggs, the great All-American BRUNCH food, are swell for that "quick n' easy" dish to serve to the noon drop-inners or the lawn-mowing husband and neighbor friends. The dishes should always win applause if you follow the few easy suggestions in this book.

Breakfast and Snack Varieties

Omelet Fines Herbes

4 eggs	2 tablespoons butter
1 teaspoon cold water	1 teaspoon chives
1 teaspoon salt	½ teaspoon rosemary
¼ teaspoon freshly ground pepper	2 teaspoons parsley

Beforehand Preparation: Blend eggs, water, salt, and pepper. Beat until creamy. Mix chives and parsley.

At the Grill: Heat a skillet. Add butter. Get butter bubbly hot. Add chives, rosemary, parsley. Cook for one minute. Add egg mixture. As eggs begin to set, move to cooler cooking quarters and lift the sides of omelet so liquid runs underneath. When omelet is nearly done return to hot spot to brown the bottom. Fold gently and serve. Start the breakfast sausages first. When finished, set aside and keep warm. While these are cooking, warm the rolls.

TRAY BOY: *butter, chives, rosemary, parsley, egg mixture*

Menu

chilled and seasoned tomato juice
omelet fines herbes
hot rolls
breakfast sausages *
coffee

Tropical Omelet

If it's been a hard night and some warmth seems to be needed in the morning, let's go for a tropical omelet:

Omelet:
3 eggs
½ teaspoon salt
a dash of pepper
1 tablespoon milk
1½ tablespoons margarine

Sauce:
1 cup canned tomatoes
1 onion finely minced
1 pimento chopped
1 tablespoon chili powder
½ teaspoon salt

Beforehand Preparation: Mash tomatoes, mince onion and pimento.

At the Grill: Make the sauce by combining all ingredients. Bring to a boil. Simmer for 15 minutes; thicken with flour if necessary. On the other side of the grill heat the skillet for the omelet. Beat eggs and add salt, pepper, and milk. Mix thoroughly. Put margarine in hot skillet. When bubbly hot, add egg mixture. As eggs begin to set, move to cooler cooking quarters and lift the sides of omelet so liquid runs underneath. When omelet is nearly done, return to hot spot to brown the bottom. Pour on sauce and fold omelet. Serves 2.

TRAY BOY: *eggs, salt, pepper, milk, margarine, tomatoes, onion, pimento, chili powder*

Menu

chilled grapefruit juice
tropical omelet
pan-fried toast
coffee

Chinese Omelet (Foo Yong)

4 eggs
¾ cup drained bean sprouts
¼ cup chopped green onions
  and tops
6 small sliced fresh mushrooms
  sliced thin—or water chestnuts, sliced thin
1 teaspoon MSG
1 tablespoon finely sliced celery
¾ cup leftover meat or seafood, chopped
3 tablespoons peanut oil
chopped parsley

Sauce:
¾ cup cream-of-chicken soup
⅓ cup water
1 teaspoon MSG
2 tablespoons soya sauce to
  taste

Beforehand Preparation: Beat eggs until lemony. Add sprouts, onions, mushrooms, MSG, and celery. Mix thoroughly and stir in meat. Beat sauce ingredients with a whisk and heat until about the consistency of heavy cream.

At the Grill: Heat a well-oiled griddle. Use a ladle and drop about ⅓ cup of mixture on griddle to make each omelet. Fry very fast until golden brown. Serve with sauce which has been kept hot. Garnish with parsley.

TRAY BOY: *egg mixture, peanut oil, sauce, parsley*

Menu

chilled pineapple juice
Chinese omelet
grilled English muffins
plum jam
coffee

Mexican-Style Scrambled Eggs

¼ cup tomato juice
2 tablespoons finely minced
 green pepper
2 tablespoons grated onion
9 eggs, beaten

½ teaspoon chili powder
1½ teaspoons salt
¼ teaspoon paprika
fat

Beforehand Preparation: Prepare vegetables, beat eggs, blend all ingredients except fat, and mix well.

At the Grill: Pour egg mixture into a hot greased skillet and slowly work backward and forward with a wooden spoon until the mixture begins to take form. While it is still loose and not too set serve hot on warmed plates. Serves 6.

TRAY BOY: *egg mixture, fat*

Menu

sliced oranges sprinkled with chopped mint
Mexican style scrambled eggs
Canadian bacon
corn muffins
coffee or tea

Gardener's Breakfast Sandwiches

After the early morning weeding you'll be ready for this tasty meal.

1 can minced ham	2 tablespoons margarine
4 tablespoons finely minced green pepper	½ teaspoon salt
2 tablespoons finely minced onion	⅛ teaspoon pepper
	4 eggs, slightly beaten
	bread

Beforehand Preparation: Chop vegetables.

At the Grill: Sauté the minced ham, pepper, and onion in the margarine until onions are soft. Season the beaten eggs and pour over mixture in the skillet. Scramble slowly until the eggs begin to set. Flip with spatula and allow another two minutes. Cut into 4 portions and serve on the toasted bread. Serves 4.

TRAY BOY: *minced ham, green pepper, onion, margarine, salt, pepper mill, eggs, bread*

Menu

fresh orange juice
gardener's breakfast sandwiches
coffee

Outdoor Breakfast

4 potatoes
4 tablespoons of bacon fat or
    margarine
1 onion
4 tablespoons green pepper
    (may be omitted)

8 tablespoons chopped ham
8 eggs
salt
pepper

Beforehand Preparation: Cut the potatoes into ½-inch cubes. Chop the onions, ham, and green pepper.

At the Grill: Place the potatoes in a skillet, cover with water, and bring to a boil. Simmer for 7 minutes. Pour off the water and remove the potatoes to a bowl. Wipe the skillet with paper towels and return to the grill. Heat the bacon fat or margarine. Mix the potatoes, onion, and green pepper. Brown them in the fat, stirring occasionally. When lightly brown add the beaten eggs, ham, salt, and pepper to taste. Scramble all together until the eggs have a moist, firm consistency. Serves 6.

TRAY BOY: *potatoes, bacon fat or margarine, onion, green pepper, eggs, chopped ham, salt, pepper*

Menu

    chilled pineapple juice
    outdoor breakfast, potatoes and eggs
    toasted rolls
    coffee

Eggs in Beer

1 can beer
4 eggs
seasoned salt
pepper

bread
butter
parsley

Beforehand Preparation: Chop parsley.

At the Grill: Pour the can of beer in a skillet and heat. Open and carefully drop the eggs into the simmering beer. Poach until firm. Toast the bread over the grill. Remove eggs carefully with a spatula. Place on buttered toast. Season with salt, pepper. Place a dab of butter on each egg. Sprinkle parsley over all. Serves 2.

> TRAY BOY: *beer, eggs, seasoned salt, pepper mill, bread, butter, parsley*

Menu

grapefruit halves sprinkled with grenadine
poached eggs on toast
grilled bacon *
tea

Stuffed Eggs

Good old deviled eggs! They are always successful finger foods for the hungry crowd to nibble while the chef completes his masterpiece. Serve them chilled on a platter surrounded by celery, carrot, and cucumber sticks. Sprig with parsley or watercress.

8 hard-cooked eggs	a dash of Tabasco sauce
1 small can deviled ham	1 tablespoon finely chopped
2 tablespoons mayonnaise	pickle
	parsley

Slice the eggs in half. Mix the yolks with ham, mayonnaise, Tabasco sauce and pickle. Fill the eggs high and "pleat" them with a fork. Garnish with parsley.

4 hard-cooked eggs	¼ teaspoon dry mustard
2 tablespoons grated sharp	¼ teaspoon Worcestershire
cheese	sauce
1 teaspoon cider vinegar	salt
2 tablespoons mayonnaise	cayenne pepper
	paprika

Mix the yolks with the other ingredients, adding salt and cayenne to taste. Fill the egg whites and dust with paprika.

4 hard-cooked eggs	½ teaspoon finely grated
2 teaspoons curry powder	lemon rind
1 teaspoon lemon juice	2 tablespoons cream
	salt and pepper
	chives

Proceed as above. Garnish with finely chopped chives.

4 hard-cooked eggs	1 teaspoon dried fine herbs
1 teaspoon lemon juice	1 teaspoon fresh chopped
2 tablespoons mustard	parsley
mayonnaise	salt and cayenne pepper
	pimento

Freshen the dried herbs by soaking in cold water for ½ hour. Proceed as above. Garnish with thin strips of pimento.

5. Sauces

Sauces are the notes upon which the true barbecue artist plays in creating his culinary symphonies. He calls at will upon robust overtones in marinading his steak—upon delicate, subtly flavored taste tones in preparing a fish sauce. Always he is a *maestro* in the art of knowing exactly the *right* sauce for every occasion!

Chart for Barbecue Sauces

Here's a chart for barbecue sauces to serve as a guide in mixing something special of your own. They all began with "dipney"—a blend of sweet country lard, salt, and the strongest vinegar, thick and hot with red and black pepper—which was used to baste the roasting meat at the all-American barbecues of the last century. Later on, other ingredients were added to improve the texture of the meat or brighten the flavor of the sauce. Now the sky's the limit. You can perform magic with the addition of herbs and spices—not to mention the handy flavored additions available at epicurean food stores.

	"Dipney" for all meats Basting sauce	Basic all-round sauce, beef, lamb, veal	Mexican	For pork	For chicken
Fat	sweet lard	2 tablespoons butter or margarine	½ cup oil or butter	fat from pork is sufficient	2 tablespoons butter or chicken fat
salt	to taste	to taste	to taste	scant	to taste
"Pepper uppers" black, white, red pepper, paprika, Tabasco	Black and cayenne	black pepper and paprika to taste	Mexican red pepper, very sparingly used	freshly ground black or white	freshly ground black or white pepper to taste
Vinegar and/or lemon juice	strong cider vinegar	¼ cup vinegar (malt or cider)	½ cup red wine, vinegar, (half water if desired)	3 tablespoons	½ cup to 1 cup white wine vinegar
Onion and garlic		⅓ cup chopped onion	1 small onion; 1 clove chopped garlic	1 small chopped onion; garlic juice	onion juice
Tomato sauce, catsup		1 cup catsup	1 cup canned tomato sauce	3 tablespoons catsup	½ cup catsup
Sugar white, brown		1 tablespoon white		2 tablespoons brown	1 teaspoon white
Mustard powdered, prepared		2 tablespoons prepared		1½ teaspoons dry	¼ teaspoon dry
Other spices and herbs			1 teaspoon chili powder	to taste	to taste
Prepared sauces			Use as directed to taste		

Basic Marinade for Meat *

1 cup vinegar
1 cup water
6 bay leaves
2 sliced carrots
1 teaspoon rosemary

1 chopped onion
1 teaspoon salt
½ teaspoon freshly ground
    pepper
1 clove mashed garlic

Cook ingredients for an hour. Soak beef, veal, or pork 24 hours before using. After use, refrigerate marinade until needed again.

Marinade for Fish

2 carrots
1 onion
1 mashed garlic bud
½ teaspoon basil
½ teaspoon marjoram
½ teaspoon savory
6 sprigs parsley

1 teaspoon butter
4 cups cider or white wine
12 cracked peppercorns
1 teaspoon allspice
½ teaspoon powdered clove
2 teaspoons salt

Simmer for 30 minutes. Poach fish in this marinade or marinate before cooking. Can be used over and over.

Marinade for Game

2 cups red wine
1 cup vinegar
2 cups water
12 cracked peppercorns

1 teaspoon powdered bay leaf
2 teaspoons sugar
1 sliced carrot
1 small chopped onion

Bring to a boil. Simmer 5 minutes. Large game should be marinated 24 hours and turned at least 4 or 5 times.

* SERVICE NOTE: *Marinade is a French culinary term meaning brine for soaking fish, flesh, or fowl.*

Marinade of Beer

3 tablespoons sugar
1 tablespoon salt
1 teaspoon cloves
dash of cayenne pepper
grated rind 1 large lemon

juice 1 large onion
½ cup salad oil
1 bottle (12 oz.) beer
2 ice cubes

Mix dry ingredients together; add ice cubes and grated lemon rind and enough beer to make a smooth paste. Add salad oil slowly, stirring rapidly. Add remainder of beer, onion juice, or finely minced onion. Pour into a pint jar with tight-fitting lid. Leave out at room temperature overnight and then store in refrigerator. This keeps indefinitely. Shake vigorously before using. An all-purpose marinade.

Herb Barbecue Sauce for Lamb

1 small onion
3 cloves garlic
2 sprigs rosemary (or 1 tea-
    spoon dried rosemary)

12 fresh mint leaves or ground
    mint
¼ cup vinegar
½ cup water

Chop onion and garlic fine and add rosemary and mint leaves which have been crushed. Add vinegar and water and let mixture stand overnight. When ready to barbecue steaks or chops, brush them thoroughly with the sauce. As the meat cooks, baste occasionally. Pass more of the same sauce when serving the lamb.

Wine Barbecue Sauce

1 cup salad oil
1 cup wine or wine vinegar
2 large onions, grated or
    minced fine

1 clove mashed garlic
1 tablespoon salt
1 teaspoon black pepper

Mix ingredients well and let stand overnight. Stir well just before using. Good for all red meats.

Barbecue Sauce à la Lucifer

3 garlic cloves, mashed
½ cup tarragon vinegar
1 tablespoon dry mustard
1 teaspoon powdered bay leaf
½ teaspoon freshly ground
  pepper
1 teaspoon paprika
1 teaspoon salt

2 small cans condensed tomato
  soup
2 bouillon cubes
2 tablespoons butter
1 teaspoon Worcestershire
  sauce
3 tablespoons A-1 sauce
a few drops Tabasco sauce

Mustard, pepper, bay leaf, salt, garlic, and paprika
are put in the vinegar and simmered down to half the quantity. Strain, then squeeze a little of the solid stuff through
strainer and add to liquid. Heat tomato soup with bouillon
cubes and butter and add strained liquid. Add Worcestershire, Tabasco and A-1 sauces. A quick-broiled affair like
Shashlik will be more worth remembering if you smear some
of this sauce on the meat before you start operations.

Savory Sauce for Steaks

2 tablespoons olive oil
1 clove garlic
½ can tomato paste
3 or 4 fillets of anchovies
2 tablespoons chopped mushrooms

1 tablespoon parsley
salt and pepper to taste
½ cup water

Brown garlic in olive oil. Remove. Dilute tomato
paste in water, combine the rest of the ingredients and simmer for 20 minutes. Add warm sauce just as you serve.

Sauce for Steak or Cold Meats

1 can tomato paste
1 tablespoon drained, grated
  horseradish
½ teaspoon dry mustard

½ teaspoon salt
½ teaspoon sugar
1 teaspoon vinegar
1 teaspoon onion juice

Mix all together. Let stand overnight. Serve cold.

Tomato—Okra Sauce

1 #2½ can tomatoes
2 cloves garlic mashed
4 cups meat stock or bouillon
2 cups thin-sliced okra
1 cup onions
1 cup sliced celery
½ teaspoon bay leaf
½ teaspoon orégano
½ teaspoon basil
½ teaspoon powdered cloves

¼ pound margarine
juice of one lemon
1 cup oil
1 cup dry white wine
½ cup Worcestershire sauce
2 teaspoons salt
½ teaspoon freshly ground
   pepper
1 tablespoon sugar
1 teaspoon chili powder

Cook the first ten ingredients for 30 minutes. Strain and add remaining ingredients. Bring to a boil and simmer gently for 15 minutes. A delicious all-round-basting-and-serving sauce which you may save for weeks in your icebox. This makes a very large quantity and should do for many barbecues.

Spanish Sauce

An eating sauce, not for basting. Good on hamburgers, frankfurters and pork.

1 minced onion
1 chopped green pepper
1 small can sliced mushrooms
2 tablespoons butter
1 #2 can tomatoes
1 tablespoon cornstarch

salt
pepper
1 tablespoon Worcestershire
   sauce
a few drops Tabasco sauce
2 tablespoons minced olives

Cook sauce ingredients slowly for 45 minutes. Thicken with cornstarch if necessary. Add Worcestershire, Tabasco, and olives. Season to taste.

Burgundy Glazing Sauce

1 small can tomato paste
2 cloves mashed garlic
¼ cup butter
1 small can tomato sauce
¼ cup honey
½ cup California Burgundy

2 limes—juice and minced peel
1 teaspoon salt
½ teaspoon freshly ground
   pepper
1 teaspoon celery salt
½ teaspoon ground ginger

Blend all ingredients and bring to a boil. Simmer gently for 15 minutes. A basting sauce which will create a beautiful shining brown finish on your roasts.

Tabasco Barbecue Sauce

1 tablespoon butter or
   margarine
1 medium onion, chopped
1 8-ounce can tomato sauce
1 tablespoon vinegar
1 tablespoon lemon juice
2 tablespoons brown sugar

1 teaspoon salt
1 teaspoon dry mustard
1 teaspoon Tabasco sauce
1 bay leaf
1 clove garlic
¼ cup water

Combine all ingredients in a saucepan. Bring to a boil. Use as a basting sauce for spareribs, chicken, or beef. Very hot.

Creole Barbecue Sauce

2 tablespoons butter
1 medium chopped onion
1 clove chopped garlic
½ cup chopped celery with
   leaves
¼ cup chopped green pepper
1 #2 can tomatoes
1 6-ounce can tomato paste
1 bay leaf

3 tablespoons brown sugar
2 teaspoons dry mustard
⅓ cup vinegar
½ teaspoon cloves
½ teaspoon allspice
2 slices lemon
1½ teaspoons salt
½ teaspoon Tabasco sauce

Melt butter; add onion and garlic; cook until tender but not brown. Add remaining ingredients; simmer 30 minutes. Let stand until cool. Strain. Use on meat loaf, chicken, spareribs, or frankfurters.

A-1 Barbecue Sauce

½ cup A-1 sauce
½ cup salad oil
1 clove mashed garlic

2 tablespoons lemon juice
½ teaspoon salt
¼ teaspoon pepper

This sauce is for basting meat, fish, or fowl. Add 2 tablespoons of finely chopped mint for lamb.

Barbecue Sauce, California-Style

1 teaspoon onion juice
¼ pound sweet butter
juice of one lemon or lime
1 teaspoon Worcestershire
    sauce

1 teaspoon MSG
1 teaspoon chopped parsley
2 tablespoons catsup
1 teaspoon dry mustard

Simmer until well-mixed, stirring occasionally. Brush the barbecue with this when turning. Use on any meat.

Colorado Barbecue Sauce

½ cup vegetable shortening
juice of 1 lemon
1 tablespoon corn syrup
1 teaspoon salt
1 teaspoon chili powder
1 teaspoon Worcestershire
    sauce

grind of fresh pepper
1 small minced onion
1 cup consommé
dash of cayenne pepper
½ teaspoon dry mustard
1 clove mashed garlic

Combine ingredients and bring to a boil. Reduce heat and simmer for a half hour. Use to marinate and baste veal, chicken, beef, and pork.

Very Special Homemade Mustard

½ cup Coleman's dry mustard
honey
vinegar (white wine vinegar is
    best)

½ teaspoon salt
⅛ teaspoon cinnamon
⅛ teaspoon ground clove

Put mustard and seasoning in a bowl and add honey until it is a thick, sticky paste. Dilute with vinegar to desired consistency. Make 24 hours before using.

Special Chili Sauce #1

1 #2 can tomatoes	1 tablespoon sugar
1 large bottle catsup	2 tablespoons chili powder
1 minced medium onion	¼ teaspoon salt

Mix thoroughly and mash until tomatoes become a pulp. Let this cook at boiling point for 30 minutes, stirring to keep from burning. This sauce is excellent on meats, fish, stews, gravies, oysters, game, and some vegetables.

Special Chili Sauce #2

1 pint fresh or canned toma- toes, mashed to a pulp	1 teaspoon minced onion
1 pint water	1 teaspoon granulated sugar
	chili powder to taste

Makes a delicious chili sauce for weiners, hamburgers, fish, oysters, and vegetables. Cook as above. This can be put up in fruit jars and kept like any other chili sauce or catsup.

Special Chili Sauce #3

3 tablespoons butter	3 tablespoons flour
2 onions, minced	1 teaspoon salt
2 finely chopped green peppers	2 tablespoons chili powder
2 cloves mashed garlic	1 #2 can tomatoes
1 tablespoon sugar	1 cup meat stock

Cook onion, green pepper, and garlic in butter until soft. Add flour, salt, chili powder, and sugar. Stir until smooth. Add tomatoes and meat stock. Cook until thickened and smooth.

Clam Sauce for Spaghetti

1 cup finely chopped clams	1 tablespoon sugar
1 chopped Bermuda onion	½ teaspoon pepper
1 clove mashed garlic	1 teaspoon ground cloves
½ cup olive oil	1 #2 can tomatoes
1 cup water	1 small can tomato paste
1 tablespoon salt	

Heat the oil in a skillet. Sauté the onions and garlic slowly until onions are transparent. Add remaining ingredients except clams. Cook for an hour. Stir from time to time. Add clams. Cook 8 minutes longer. Pour over hot spaghetti. Pass a dish of grated Parmesan cheese. Serves 6.

Chart for Spices, Seeds and Herbs

A wise man once said that you can judge the quality of a man's mind by his bookshelf and the quality of a woman's cooking by her spice shelf. Two meals produced with the same facilities can be as different as wine and water. The difference is the narrow margin of a few pinches of seasoning and the ability to follow a recipe.

We hope this chart will be a helpful guide.

Name	Use With
allspice (pimento) *spice*	pickling, meats, gravy, boiling fish, baking, puddings, relishes
anise *seed*	cookies, candies, sweet pickles, beverages, coffee cakes, rolls, fruit pies
basil (sweet basil) *herb*	tomato dishes, peas, squash, string beans, omelet, lamb chops, turtle soup, venison, duck
bay leaves (laurel) *herb*	pickling, stews, soups, fish, chowder, fish kebab, shish kebab, marinades
caraway *seed*	rye bread, sauerkraut, new cabbage, noodles, soft cheese spreads, French-fried potatoes, pork, liver, kidneys
cardamom *seed*	pickling, demi-tasse, coffee cakes, grape jelly, melon
cinnamon *spice*	preserving, puddings, stewed fruits, chocolate sauce, baked goods, sweet potatoes
cayenne (chili pepper) *condiment*	meats, sauces, fish, egg dishes
celery salt *condiment*	eggs, potato salad, salad dressings, tomato and sauerkraut juices, bouillon
celery seed *seed*	pickling, cole slaw, fish, salad dressings, vegetables
chervil *herb*	soups, salads, egg dishes, French dressing, fish, butter sauce for chicken, garnish
chili powder *blend*	chili con carne, shellfish and oyster cocktail sauces, boiled and scrambled eggs, gravy, stew seasoning, hamburgers
cloves *spice*	pork and ham roasts, pickling of fruit, spiced sweet syrups, chocolate pudding, stews, curry, marinades
coriander *seed*	frankfurters, game sauce, cookies, cakes, biscuits, poultry stuffings, mixed green salads, pork, sausages

Name	Use With
cumin *seed*	soups, cheese, pies, stuffed eggs and many Mexican dishes
curry powder *blend*	eggs, vegetables, fish, French dressing, scalloped tomatoes, clam and fish chowders, spareribs
dill *seed*	guacamole, lamb stew, sauerkraut, soups, fish and meat sauces, vinegars
fennel *seed*	lentils, sweet pickles, boiled fish, pastries, candies, liquors
ginger *spice*	chutneys, curries, conserves, pickling, applesauce, fruit compote, gingerbread, pumpkin pie, Indian pudding, canned fruits, pot roast, chicken, and other meats
mace *spice*	fish sauces, pickling, preserving, chocolate dishes, whipped cream
marjoram *herb*	stews, soups, veal, eggs, tomatoes, sausage, poultry seasonings, fish, sauces
mint (dried) *herb*	lamb, carrots, peas, zucchini, beverages, fruit, salads, garnish
mustard *seed*	prepared mustard, salads, pickled meats, fish, hamburgers, frankfurters, sauces, gravies
nutmeg *spice*	puddings, eggnog, custards, whipped cream, spinach, fried bananas
orégano *herb*	guacamole, marinades, pheasant, guinea hen, meat sauces, gravies, eggs, spaghetti
paprika *spice*	a garnish on chicken paprika and Hungarian goulash, fish, shellfish, salad dressings, vegetables, meats, gravy, canapés
parsley dried *herb*	garnish on soups, salads, meat, fish, sauces, potatoes
pepper *spice*	meats, sauces, gravy, vegetables, soups, salads, eggs, curing hams
poppy *seed*	garnish on canapés, breads, rolls, cookies, salads, noodles, pastries
rosemary *herb*	soups, lamb, wild fowl, duck, rabbit, stews, meat stocks
saffron *spice*	cookies, cakes, rice, bouillabaisse
sage *herb*	sausages, meat or poultry, stuffings, baked fish, green salads
savory *herb*	hamburgers, meat dressings, chicken, fish, pork, scrambled eggs, beans
sesame *seed*	rolls, buns, potatoes, candy

Chart for Spices, Seeds and Herbs—Continued

Name	Use With
tarragon *herb*	salads, chicken, veal, sweet breads, fish sauce, lobster, egg, tomato dishes
thyme *herb*	stews, soups, poultry, mutton, venison, veal, stuffings, clam and fish chowders, fish sauces, fricassees
turmeric *spice*	prepared mustard, chow-chow relish, curry dishes

6. Salads

Americans, especially Californians, excel in the art of salad making. Colorful, zesty salads offer the barbecue expert an enjoyable opportunity for showmanship in preparing the *balancing* part of a meal. Wise indeed is he who takes special care to create salads that have both taste and eye appeal. Try some in this chapter . . . you will be amazed at the results.

Salade Comme Il Faut

1 head lettuce
1 teaspoon salt
¼ teaspoon pepper
2 tablespoons vinegar

6 tablespoons olive oil
garlic and small cubes stale
bread

Separate the leaves of lettuce and wash each thoroughly. Shake out water and wrap in a clean towel or several thicknesses of cheese-cloth. Wrap closely and chill until needed. Put leaves in a large salad bowl, breaking large leaves into small pieces with the fingers. Do not cut with a knife. Sprinkle on salt and toss with wooden fork and spoon. Then add pepper, oil, and finally vinegar. If garlic flavor is desired, rub crushed clove of garlic on bread crust and put in bowl. Remove and discard after salad is mixed. If salad is sufficiently tossed, there will be no salad dressing in bottom of bowl. Freshly dressed salad is usually preferred, but some guests may prefer the "tired" variety—salade fatiguée. To make this, greens should be dressed an hour or two ahead of time and allowed to marinate before serving. Serves 4.

Chef's Salad

1 head of Boston lettuce
1 bunch of watercress
1 bunch of romaine
1 head of chicory
freshly ground pepper
1 clove garlic

¼ cup each cut in thin
  slivers: chicken, salami
  (tongue or ham may be
  substituted), cheese
3 tablespoons red wine vinegar
9 tablespoons oil
½ teaspoon salt
¼ teaspoon paprika

Buy fresh, crisp greens. Clean them carefully, using a lettuce basket. Shake dry. Place in a bag. Crisp in the refrigerator. Rub the wooden bowl with a cut clove of garlic. Tear the leaves apart with your fingers. Add the meat and cheese. Season generously with fresh coarse-ground pepper. Mix the oil, vinegar, paprika, and salt, shaking hard in a bottle. Just before serving add the dressing a little at a time; toss lightly until each leaf is nicely coated with dressing. No surplus dressing should ever be left in the bottom of the bowl. Serves 8–10.

Caesar Salad *(California's finest)*

2 cloves garlic
3 tablespoons olive oil
2 cups white-bread croutons
2 eggs
2 heads tender romaine
¼ teaspoon dry mustard
½ teaspoon salt

¼ teaspoon freshly ground coarse pepper
¼ pound bleu cheese
4 anchovy fillets chopped fine
7 tablespoons olive oil
juice of medium lemon
2 tablespoons red wine vinegar

Mash one garlic clove through garlic press. Mix into 3 tablespoons olive oil in a skillet. Fry croutons in oil until golden brown all over. Drop eggs into boiling water. Turn off heat. Let them stand 3 minutes. Remove and cool. Mix oil, salt, pepper, and mustard. Rub a large wooden salad bowl with a cut clove of garlic. Tear romaine by hand into bite-size pieces. Break eggs over greens. Add crumbled bleu cheese and chopped anchovies (anchovies are optional, since some people are not over-fond of them). Sprinkle with oil, then vinegar and lemon juice. Toss thoroughly with wooden servers. Too much strength will wilt the leaves, so be gentle. At the last minute before serving, drop croutons over all and toss salad just enough to mix. Serve this as a good companion to food from the grill or as a solo dish for luncheon.

Cucumber-and-Sour-Cream Salad

2 medium-sized cucumbers
1 teaspoon of salt
1 head of iceberg lettuce

1 pint of sour cream
1½ teaspoons of onion juice
paprika

Slice cucumbers very thin and sprinkle with salt. Let them stand for ½ hour. Shred the head of lettuce into a fine slaw. Place in a bowl with the cucumbers. Cover and chill. When ready to serve, mix the sour cream and onion juice. Pour over the salad. Garnish with paprika and rosettes of unpared sliced cucumber. Excellent with fish.

Cole Slaw with Cream Dressing

1 large head of young cabbage
1 minced green pepper
1 teaspoon salt
¼ teaspoon pepper
2 tablespoons sugar

⅛ teaspoon paprika
1 cup sour cream
⅓ cup tarragon vinegar
crisp lettuce leaves

Finely shred the cabbage and soak in ice water for 30 minutes. Drain. Add the vinegar, salt, pepper, sugar and paprika. Toss and place in the refrigerator for 1 hour. Add the green pepper. Toss again. Stir in the sour cream. Mix thoroughly. Arrange in crisp lettuce cups. Garnish with paprika and serve cold. Chopped apple or pineapple can be substituted for the green pepper. Serves 8-12.

Tossed Cabbage Salad

1 small head of young cabbage
⅓ cup thinly sliced onion
½ cup chopped parsley
1 small can chopped pimentos
¼ cup salad oil

2 tablespoons basil vinegar
2 tablespoons sugar
¼ teaspoon cracked pepper
1 teaspoon salt

Shred the cabbage very fine. Add the onions, parsley, and pimentos. Chill in the refrigerator. Combine the oil, vinegar, sugar, pepper, and salt. Shake well. Line the salad bowl with green cabbage leaves. Fill with salad and pour on the dressing. Toss lightly. Serves 6.

Combination Vegetable Salad

cooked carrots
cooked beets
cooked string beans
cooked peas
cooked cauliflower buds
cooked celery
cooked lima beans

cooked white turnips
cooked asparagus tips
cooked artichoke hearts
cooked corn
dressing
lettuce
chives

Select 4 or more vegetables from this list to make 4 cups. Leftovers may be used. Combine with French dressing or mayonnaise to the desired consistency. Place on crisp lettuce. Garnish with chopped chives. Serves 6.

Chiffonade Salad

1 tender head romaine
1 tender head lettuce
1 tender head escarole
4 stalks celery cut in long, thin slices

2 tomatoes, quartered
½ cup sliced pickled beets
1 hard-cooked egg, chopped
watercress

Wash greens and celery and tear into bite-size pieces. Mix with tomatoes and beets. Stir finely chopped chives and finely chopped egg into chiffonade dressing. Pour over. Mix salad well and serve.

Pick-and-Choose Salad

Choose what you wish to serve from this list:

Greens:
heads of lettuce
heads of chicory
heads of romaine
slivers of sweet green and red
    pepper
Bermuda onion, sliced paper
    thin
tender young spinach leaves
finocchio
cooked zucchini discs
endive spears
cooked green beans
slices of cucumber

Solids:
wedges of tomatoes
wedges of hard-boiled egg
radishes
assorted olives
flowerettes of raw cauliflower
anchovy fillets
carrot sticks
celery sticks
gherkins

To make it easy for your guests, have two salad bowls, one rubbed with garlic for the leafy greens and another for the solid pieces. Have several 10-inch skewers beside each bowl, a cruet of French dressing, a pepper and a salt mill handy. Arrange the food for color contrast in ribbons or orderly groups. Each person picks his own combination of greens and solids, spearing them on a skewer and depositing on his salad plate, adding seasoning and dressing to taste.

Salad That Has Almost Everything (marvelous to serve with hamburgers or frankfurters)

½ cup shredded ham
½ cup finely sliced celery
1 head tender leafy lettuce
1 head romaine
1 cup canned grapefruit
    sections
½ cup French dressing
4 hard-cooked eggs
2 tablespoons chopped parsley

Just before serving, place everything but eggs, parsley, and dressing in bowl. Pour on dressing and toss. Garnish with hard-cooked egg and parsley.

Fiesta Salad

3 eggs
2 cups each chopped celery
  and red cabbage
3 cups cubed cooked potatoes
1 tablespoon chopped onion

4 tablespoons chopped sweet
  cucumber pickle
2 tablespoons chopped parsley
1 teaspoon chili powder
1 cup mayonnaise
lettuce

Boil eggs, chill under running water, remove shells and chop. Prepare chopped vegetables and potato cubes. Wash and chill lettuce. Arrange border of lettuce in salad bowl. Mix chopped ingredients with mayonnaise. Pile in the salad bowl and sprinkle with chili powder. A good side dish to serve with steak, hamburgers, or shashlik.

Macaroni Salad

1¼ cup elbow macaroni
1 cup diced tomatoes
½ cup minced green pepper
1 cup diced celery
3 diced sweet gherkins

1½ to 2 teaspoons salt
½ cup mayonnaise
½ cup beer
1 teaspoon celery seed
3 hard-cooked eggs

Cook macaroni in boiling water until tender. Drain and rinse in cold water. Chill. Combine macaroni, tomatoes, green pepper, celery, and gherkins. Combine salt, mayonnaise, beer, and celery seed; add to macaroni mixture; mix well. Chill several hours. Serve on lettuce and garnish with hard-cooked eggs. 6 servings.

Macaroni Doodad Salad

1 cup cooked macaroni
¼ cup cooked peas
¼ cup shredded carrot
¼ cup chopped salami

1 teaspoon finely minced
  onion
½ cup mayonnaise
lettuce or cabbage leaves
paprika

Lightly mix all the solid ingredients. Add the mayonnaise and stir in thoroughly. Add more mayonnaise if necessary. Serve on crisp lettuce or cabbage cups. Sprinkle with paprika. Serves 4.

Special Potato Salad

⅔ cup mayonnaise
¼ cup beer
½ cup finely chopped sweet
    pickles

1 teaspoon celery seed
4 cups cubed cooked potatoes
salt and pepper

Combine mayonnaise, beer, pickles, and celery seed; add to potatoes and mix well. Season to taste with salt and pepper. Chill. Serve on salad greens. Serves 6.

Old-Fashioned Potato Salad

8 medium-sized potatoes
1 tablespoon salt
½ cup finely cut celery
2 tablespoons chopped parsley
2 green onions
1 cup mayonnaise

1 teaspoon salt
1½ teaspoons sugar
2 tablespoons dill vinegar
2 hard-cooked eggs
sprigs of parsley

Beforehand Preparation: Scrub potatoes of equal size. Cover with cold water, add salt, cover, and bring to a boil. Lower the heat. Do not overcook. Remove from the fire when barely done. Peel and cut into ¾-inch cubes. Add celery, parsley, and onions. Mix mayonnaise, salt, sugar and vinegar. While the potatoes are still warm, pour on the dressing and mix. Let stand at room temperature for 15 minutes so that the warm potatoes will absorb the dressing. Garnish with slices of hard-cooked egg and parsley. Chill. Serve 8.

Avocado-and-Seedless-Grape Salad

2 avocados
½ pound seedless grapes

⅓ cup tart French dressing
lemon juice

Slice the grapes in half. Marinate in the refrigerator for 1 hour in French dressing. Cut the chilled avocados in half, sprinkle with lemon. Fill with grapes and dressing. Serves 4.

Southern Fruit Salad

1 cup pared diced peaches	salt
1 cup unpared diced apples	cayenne
2 peeled and diced bananas	½ lemon
1 grapefruit in skinless sections	creamy dressing
1 cup halved seedless grapes	

Save the juice of the fruit as you prepare it. Add to fruit in a glass bowl. Squeeze lemon juice over all. Mix. Place on lettuce and pour over a rich creamy dressing to which a little pineapple juice has been added. Garnish with mint. Serves 6.

Chart for French Dressing

The chart shows some of the standard salad dressings derived from basic French Dressing. They all started from the essential ingredients of oil, vinegar, salt, and pepper. For a richer dressing use more oil—up to five parts oil to one part vinegar. For a sharper sauce, use more vinegar, or substitute lemon or other citrus fruit for all or part. Use any good vegetable oil or olive oil. Use the chart for quick reference or as a starting place for your own invention. Let your conscience and good taste be your guide. Who knows, you may be the one to give the world something as tantalizing as "aux fines herbes" or chiffonade!

VARIETIES OF FRENCH DRESSING

	Oil	Vinegar	Salt	Pepper	Other Ingredients
Basic French dressing	6 tablespoons	3 tablespoons	1 tablespoon	¼ teaspoon	
Aux Fines Herbes		Tarragon vinegar			1 to 2 tablespoons each chopped chervil, chives, and parsley
Breton	substitute 6 tablespoons hot bacon fat	cider vinegar	(Mix in pan while bacon is hot, add pepper and salt, and pour over dandelion greens or green lettuce)		
Californian		Substitute grapefruit juice	Use less salt		
Chiffonade		Tarragon vinegar			2 tablespoons each chopped parsley and sweet red pepper; 2 chopped hard-cooked eggs; ½ teaspoon chopped shallot
Parisian					½ teaspoon powdered sugar; 2 teaspoons chopped mild onion; ½ tablespoon each chopped pimento and green pepper

	Vinegar	Other Ingredients
Puerto Rican	Use half lemon juice and half vinegar	2 tablespoons chopped olives; 1 tablespoon catsup
Roquefort cheese		½ cup crumbled Roquefort cheese; 3 drops onion juice
Russian		2 tablespoons chili sauce; 1 tablespoon chopped green pepper; 3 drops onion juice
Vinaigrette		1 teaspoon prepared mustard; ½ teaspoon each chopped parsley and shallot; 1 teaspoon each chopped capers and sour cucumber pickle
Western	Use half lemon and half vinegar or all lemon juice	1 tablespoon powdered sugar; 1 teaspoon catsup; ¼ teaspoon dry mustard; 2 drops Tabasco sauce

Mayonnaise Chart

The chart on the following page takes the mayonnaise for granted, for unless you're an ultra-gourmet or reactionary, you buy it in a jar. If not, you know how to make it anyway, or know someone who does it for you. The big difference between French dressing and mayonnaise is that mayonnaise starts with an egg, and the trick comes in persuading that egg yolk to absorb oil, vinegar, and/or lemon juice, salt, pepper, etc., and come up smiling, holding its shape like a Victorian lady. So let's assume that you've got the mayonnaise. The chart shows proportions for one cup.

To Make Mayonnaise	Add to One Cup Mayonnaise	Use With
aux Fines Herbes	1 tablespoon each chopped chervil, chives, tarragon, and parsley	cold fish, meat, or vegetable salads
Bar-le-Duc	½ cup heavy cream whipped; 1 tablespoon or more bar-le-duc jelly	fruit salads
East Indian	1½ tablespoons chopped chutney sauce	cold meats or as sandwich spread
Horseradish	¼ cup sour cream; 3 tablespoons drained horseradish; 1 tablespoon chopped parsley	cold beef, vegetable salads
Piquante	2 tablespoons each chopped olives and chopped capers	cold lamb or chicken, chicken salad
Pacific Island	¼ cup finely chopped blanched almonds; ¼ cup currant jelly; 3 or 4 tablespoons whipped cream	fruit salads
Rouge or Cardinal	Ground lobster coral—enough to give red tinge	fish or cucumber salads
Russian †	¼ to ½ cup well-drained chili sauce; 2 tablespoons each chopped celery, green pepper, and pimento; 1 tablespoon chopped chives or onion; ½ tablespoon chopped capers, if desired	cold meat, fish, or vegetable salad
Spanish	1 to 2 tablespoons chopped sweet red pepper; ½ clove crushed garlic; 1 tablespoon chili sauce; ½ tablespoon tarragon	cold meats, meat or vegetable salad, or as sandwich spread
Thousand Island †	Add ¼ cup heavy cream whipped stiff to Russian dressing, omitting any other ingredients to suit taste	mixed-vegetable salad or as sandwich spread. Very good with egg salad

† Neither amateurs nor experts agree as to what really constitutes the difference between Russian dressing and Thousand Island dressing. It's our well-considered opinion that the whipped cream makes the difference.

7. *Appetizers*

Toss a bone to the famished wolves while you do your stuff at the grill. Give them just enough to hold them in abeyance but not too much to spoil their appetites.

The Tide-Over Course

Raw-Vegetable Platter for Nibblers

This type of platter covers the hors d'oeuvres and the salad course. If you wish to keep the raw vegetables fresh, cover with chips of ice whenever they begin to wilt. This works wonders within a few minutes. Arrangement is half the show. Either group vegetables into a sunburst effect with a colorful heap of tiny green tomatoes, radishes, pickled beets, or stuffed olives in the center, or make broken ribbons march down the dish. Place containers of salt, pepper, seasoned salt, a cruet of French dressing, and a dunking bowl, if desired, beside the platter. Crisp cocktail tidbits, such as tiny pretzels, crackers, or salted nuts, are complementary and help fill in until meal time.

Choose your platter from this list of suggestions:

carrot sticks	pickled beets
celery curls	cooked zucchini discs
stuffed celery	slices or wedges of tomato
cucumber sticks	tiny red or green tomatoes
tiny green onions	wedges of lettuce
sliced Bermuda onions	a variety of pickles
radish rosettes	ripe and green olives
cauliflower buds	giant stuffed olives

Garnish with chopped chives, chopped parsley, or fat sprigs of watercress.

Shellfish Platter for Nibblers

Place a cabbage or grapefruit in the center of a platter and make a porcupine of shrimp, crab chunks, pickled oysters, marinated mushrooms, lobster chunks, or olives on toothpicks. Make a pleasing food picture on the platter of anchovies, stuffed eggs, strips of marinated herring, smoked salmon, sardines or smoked mussels (your choice, not all of the above, please!) Garnish with cucumber discs, lettuce curls, watercress, or egg slices.

Smörgåsbord Spread

The Swedish smörgåsbord is always served with three or four hot dishes. This summer variety has none. The hot foods are to be cooked by the guests on skewers. A wonderful, lazy party for the dog days of July and August.

Have a platter of your favorite frankfurters and skewers ready for grilling, and a table loaded with a selection from the following list:

shrimps marinated in salad dressing	chunks of cheese
potato salad	pickled beets
sliced cold cervalet or other luncheon meat	various pickles and relishes
	Ry-Krisp
sardines with lemon	pumpernickel
stuffed egg	bowl of fruit
cottage cheese mixed with horseradish	coffee
	beer

Antipasto Platter

Serve your own combination, thoroughly chilled:

canned pimento cut in squares;

ripe olives, pitted and seasoned overnight in brine with a cut clove of garlic;

celery curls or cooked celery hearts which have been marinated in French dressing;

pickled mushrooms (canned mushroom caps marinated in garlic wine vinegar);

sautéed mushrooms cooked in butter with a bay leaf, pepper, and salt;

hard-cooked eggs cut in half and decorated with strips of pimento;

anchovy fillets, capers, strips of canned red and green peppers;

artichoke hearts in oil (canned);

pickled beets; hot vinegar peppers;

tomato slices;

herring;

thin slices of salami or bologna shaped into cones.

Canteloupe and Prosciutto

1 small canteloupe
½ pound thinly cut prosciutto (Italian ham)

Chill the melon. Cut in half and remove seeds. Cut each half into long quarters. Pare. Arrange 1 slice prosciutto on each slice of melon. Serves 4.

Marinated Mushroom Hors d'Oeuvre (from Rotisserie Perigourdine in Paris)

½ pound mushrooms
salt and pepper
⅓ cup olive oil

2 tablespoons chopped parsley
juice of 1 lemon

When the large choice mushrooms are in season, this makes a lovely, fresh-tasting, before-dinner snack. Without removing the stems, cut the mushrooms very thin. Arrange in an attractive series of circles. Sprinkle with salt and freshly ground pepper. Add olive oil to coat (not too much). Sprinkle finely chopped parsley over all. Squeeze on lemon juice. Marinate in refrigerator for one hour, transfer to small plates, and serve with cocktail wafers. Serves 4.

Shrimp Rémoulade (a famous New Orleans recipe)

2 pounds cleaned shrimp
1 bay leaf
1 onion
1 clove mashed garlic
⅛ teaspoon cayenne pepper
2 tablespoons celery

1 green onion
4 tablespoons olive oil
1½ tablespoons creole mustard
¼ teaspoon paprika
2 chopped hard-boiled eggs

Boil the shrimp in water to cover seasoned with garlic, onion, bay leaf and cayenne pepper. Drain. Chop celery and green onion until fine. Add the oil, creole mustard and paprika. Mix well. Cut the shrimps in halves or thirds and mix into the sauce. Marinate in the refrigerator for three hours before serving. Garnish with chopped eggs and serve on lettuce leaves as an hors d'oeuvre. Serves 6.

Angels on Horseback

8 large cooked prunes
8 small oysters
8 pieces bacon

Fill each prune with an oyster and wrap with bacon. Impale on skewers and broil over coals until bacon is crisp. Serves 4.

As the taste buds become tantalizingly stimulated, these tidbits will seem like manna from heaven while your guests are waiting for the steak or roast.

Fireside Popcorn

No sense in wasting good cooking heat while waiting for the flames to die down. Put a cup of popcorn in a long-handled wire popper. Pour on a little oil. Shuffle around. Shake over the fire until the corn becomes white and fluffy. Sprinkle with salt and melted butter or garlic butter. Serve to hold ravenous appetites in check.

Minced-Clam-and-Cream-Cheese Dunking Sauce

½ pound cream cheese
1 clove garlic
½ teaspoon celery salt
2 tablespoons of lime juice
1 can (7-8 ounces) of minced clams

½ juice from can of clams
salt
½ teaspoon Worcestershire sauce
Tabasco or hot pepper sauce

Mix the cheese, lime juice, and clam juice to a creamy consistency. Mash the garlic through a garlic press. Add the garlic pulp, celery salt, salt, Worcestershire sauce, and pepper sauce. Mix thoroughly and stir in the clams.

Serve with potato chips, celery, carrot strips, or melba toast.

Avocado Dunking Mix

1 large ripe avocado
juice of ½ a lemon or lime
½ cup sour or sweet cream
salt

pepper
1 teaspoon curry powder
½ teaspoon garlic salt

Slice the top from the avocado, leaving the best two-thirds of the shell intact. Carefully remove the seed and discard. Scoop out the meat and sprinkle with lemon juice. Add sour cream, curry powder, and garlic salt. Mash with a fork until all lumps disappear. Season with salt and freshly ground pepper to taste. Serve in the avocado shell with potato chips, crackers, or Ry-Krisp on the side.

Guacamole

The present rage in appetizers, which has taken too long getting here from Old Mexico.

2 large ripe avocados
2 tablespoons grated onion
juice ½ lemon
1 teaspoon wine vinegar
1 teaspoon salt

¼ teaspoon pepper
1 ripe tomato, chopped
1 small chili, chopped
1 teaspoon oil

Slice avocados in half. Sprinkle meat with lemon juice. Mash until creamy. The easiest way is to put it through a sieve. Add remaining ingredients. Mix well. Serve chilled with crisp wafers or as a sauce for meat, fish, vegetables, or rice.

Shrimp Dunking Sauce

Good with raw vegetables, potato chips, or lettuce salad.

6 ounces of cooked shrimp
½ pint of sour cream
1 teaspoon horseradish
1 teaspoon lime juice

1 teaspoon Worcestershire sauce
½ teaspoon salt
¼ cup catsup
½ teaspoon dry mustard

Pour all the ingredients in the order listed into your electric mixer or chop the shrimp to small bits, and use a hand beater. Blend the ingredients thoroughly. Chill. Serve in a dish in the center of a platter of raw vegetables cut in strips or bite-sized pieces

A quick salad to serve; cut firm heads of iceberg lettuce into quarters or sixths depending on size. Serve with generous quantities of the shrimp sauce.

8.
Vegetables

Most colorful substance of the food world is the vegetable kingdom. While the legumes and roots play second fiddle to the serious business of Main Course Overtures, they add the necessary undertone of harmony to balance the meal and remove the edge from ravenous outdoor appetites.

POTATOES, VEGETABLES AND
VARIOUS FARINACEOUS DISHES

Hashed Brown Potatoes

4 tablespoons of bacon fat
3 cups of finely chopped or
   diced cooked potatoes
½ teaspoon of salt

¼ teaspoon of freshly ground
   pepper
¼ teaspoon of onion or garlic
   salt

Beforehand Preparation: Mix the potatoes and seasonings in a bowl.

At the Grill: Heat the fat on a griddle and add the potatoes. Press them down with a spatula into a cake about 1 inch thick. Cook them until the underside is crispy and a rich brown. Using the spatula, loosen the potatoes from the bottom. Now flip the cake over in one piece. Brown the other side and serve. Catsup is sometimes served with hashed brown potatoes.

TRAY BOY: *seasoned potatoes, fat*

Menu

hashed-brown potatoes
hamburgers—your favorite way
platter of fresh vegetables with dunking sauce
baking-powder biscuits
apple pie and cheese
coffee or cola drinks

Charcrust Baked Potatoes

Scrub potatoes well and soak in hot water for one minute. While still wet, roll potatoes in CHARCRUST and roast on the grill, turning until tender. Eat jacket and all.

Roasted Potatoes and Onions

Potatoes or onions may be buried in coals in their skins, or a coating of clay or mud may be applied before roasting. When they are done, the coating falls off and the vegetables are delicious. While cooking, level embers so that food cooks evenly all around. Change position halfway through roasting. Roasting time will be about 55 minutes. Serve with plenty of butter, salt, and a filled pepper mill.

Roasting or grill surface requires a metal dome or portable oven. Turn often until done when tested. Rubbing potato skins with fat and salt makes edible jackets that are crisp and tasty. Try a sprinkle of parsley or chives—a gustatory pleasure.

Puffy Corn Oysters

2 cups fresh corn kernels	1 teaspoon baking powder
2 beaten egg yolks	a pinch of nutmeg
¾ cup flour	2 egg whites, beaten stiff
1 teaspoon salt	maple syrup
¼ teaspoon pepper	fat

Beforehand Preparation: Grate the corn from the cob on a coarse grater. Add beaten egg yolks, sifted flour, salt, pepper, nutmeg, and baking powder, and mix thoroughly. Gently fold in the egg whites.

At the Grill: Drop by teaspoonfuls into 1 inch of hot fat. Brown on both sides. Eat at once with hot maple syrup or honey. Serves 4.

TRAY BOY: *corn batter, fat, hot syrup*

Menu

raspberries and cream
corn oysters
hot syrup
breakfast sausages *
coffee

Boiled Corn on the Cob

12 unhusked ears of corn   salt
2 tablespoons sugar   pepper mill
butter

Buy the corn from a reliable green grocer as close to eating time as possible or pluck it from your own garden, if you happen to be so lucky, a few minutes before boiling. Husk and beard the ears and plop them one by one into a big kettle of fiercely boiling water. Add sugar and cook about 7 minutes, or until tender. Serve at once with plenty of butter, salt, and freshly ground pepper. Truly the all-American summer feast.

Corn Jamboree

Clean all but the white layer of husk from 2 packs of corn. Place in steamer or kettle over a wood or charcoal fire. Steam for 30 minutes. Serve with plenty of butter, salt, and pepper. Cold fried chicken and a crisp green salad will fill out the rest of the meal.

Corn Roasted Over the Coals

    8 ears of freshly picked corn with long nubs
    butter
    salt
    pepper

Beforehand Preparation: Pull husks aside a little and soak the unhusked corn in salt water for an hour. Shake well before roasting.

At the Grill: The unhusked corn can be placed directly in the burned-down ashes. Level the embers around the corn so that it is cooked evenly all around. Change the position halfway through roasting. Leave it buried for 30 minutes. *Or* place the unhusked ears on your grill with the nubs over the end for easy handling. Roll on the grid until nicely browned —about 8 or 10 minutes. Remove the husks and serve at once with lots of salt, pepper, and butter. Serves 4.

    TRAY BOY: *corn, butter, salt, pepper*

Menu

    roasted corn
    grilled bacon on toasted buttered rolls *
    ice cream with sliced fresh peaches
    beverage

Savory Corn

3 cups cut corn—fresh, canned, or frozen
2 tablespoons chopped onion, green pepper, and pimento

3 tablespoons butter
salt and pepper to taste

If you are using fresh corn, cut it from the cob and chop onion, pepper and pimento. Melt butter in skillet and add vegetables. Cook 8 or 9 minutes, stirring to keep from sticking. If desired, a little tomato juice may be added. Season and serve hot.

Succotash

2 cups fresh corn kernels
2 cups fresh lima beans
2 tablespoons margarine
1 teaspoon salt

½ teaspoon freshly ground
  pepper
½ cup light cream

Cook separately and drain the corn and limas. Combine vegetables, margarine and seasonings. Pour on cream. Heat thoroughly. Do not boil. Serve hot. 6 portions.

Tomatoes, String Beans, and Scallions in a Skillet

6 medium-size tomatoes
¼ cup margarine
1 package frozen frenched
  string beans

6 green onions
1 teaspoon salt
pepper mill

Thaw the beans. Dip the tomatoes in boiling water for a minute and peel. Slice the onions and tops into small pieces. Melt the margarine in a skillet and add the tomatoes. Cover. Cook for 5 minutes, sprinkle with salt and freshly ground pepper. Add the onions and string beans. Cover again. Total cooking time 30 minutes. Serves 6.

Fried Tomatoes

4 tomatoes
2 eggs
2 teaspoons salt
½ teaspoon pepper
1 teaspoon curry powder

1 teaspoon water
2 tablespoons butter or
  margarine
1 cup fine cracker crumbs

Clean and cut tomatoes into ½-inch slices. Beat eggs slightly. Season with salt, pepper, and curry powder. Add water. Dip the tomato slices in egg mixture and then into the cracker crumbs. Heat the butter on a flat griddle over the barbecue and fry each slice until golden brown on both sides. Serve at once. Serves 6.

Onion Soup Provençal

4 large red onions	2 cups beer
6 tablespoons butter or	salt
margarine	pepper
3 cups of chicken stock	6 slices of toasted French bread
dash of Maggi seasoning	½ cup grated Parmesan cheese

Beforehand Preparation: Peel onions, slice thin.

At the Grill: Heat the butter or margarine in a heavy pot. Cook the onions until soft and golden brown. Add chicken stock, Maggi seasoning and beer. Simmer covered for 45 minutes. Season to taste with salt and freshly ground pepper. Pour into soup bowls. Top with toast slices. Sprinkle generously with Parmesan cheese. Serves 6.

TRAY BOY: *onions, butter or margarine, stock, Maggi seasoning, beer, salt, pepper mill, bread, Parmesan cheese*

Menu

onion soup provençal
hot dogs in togs *
tossed lettuce and tomato salad
assorted fruits and cheese
beverage

French-Fried Onion Rings

3 large mild onions, sliced ¼	1 cup flour
inch thick	1 egg beaten
¼ teaspoon baking powder	1 cup milk
1 teaspoon salt	

Make a batter of egg and milk. Soak onion rings in batter. Stir with fork until all are wet. Mix flour, salt, and baking powder. Dip onion rings in batter and fry in small batches in deep fat. Keep separated with fork. When golden brown, drain on paper toweling. Serve hot. A gorgeous accompaniment with charcoal-broiled steak. Serves 6.

Savory Kidney Beans

1 #2 can kidney beans
2 tablespoons bacon fat
1 small minced onion
1 small minced green pepper

salt
pepper
1 tablespoon red wine vinegar
3 hard-cooked eggs

Heat fat in skillet. Sauté onions and green pepper until onion is transparent. Add beans and juice, vinegar, salt and pepper to taste. Simmer 15 minutes. Serve on hot plates as a luncheon dish. Garnish with quarters of egg. Serves 4.

SERVICE NOTE: *An ideal side dish to go along with 'burgers or franks; or a good potato substitute with any meal.*

Lentils with Onions and Bacon (a tummy filler)

6 slices bacon
8 green onions with tops

1 teaspoon parsley
3 cups cooked lentils

Chop onions and parsley. Fry bacon until crisp and remove from pan. Add green onions to fat in pan and sauté until soft. Add parsley and fry the last 5 minutes. Add lentils and heat through. Crumble bacon and sprinkle over all. Serve very hot. Serves 6.

Zucchini Al Fresco

6 small zucchini squash
2 tablespoons minced onion
2 tablespoons butter or
  margarine
1½ cups tomatoes

1 teaspoon salt
¼ teaspoon pepper
½ teaspoon basil
¼ teaspoon thyme

Heat the butter or margarine in a heavy saucepan and brown the onion. Add tomatoes; simmer ten minutes. Stir in salt, pepper, basil, and thyme. Wash but do not pare zucchini. Cut into thick discs. Add to tomatoes. Cook until zucchini is tender (about 20 minutes). Serves 4.

French-Fried Zucchini

4 medium-size zucchini	¾ cup sifted flour
2 egg yolks	1 teaspoon salt
½ cup milk	1 cup shortening

Cut zucchini lengthwise in three strips. Make a batter of egg yolks, milk, flour, and salt. Dip slices in batter. Heat shortening in a skillet and fry until golden brown. Serves 4.

Zucchini

4 medium zucchini
salt

Wash zucchini but do not peel. Cut in discs ½ inch thick. Boil in salted water until tender (about 7 minutes).

Serve hot with a spoonful of sour cream or a sprinkle of lemon juice.

For zucchini parmigiane place zucchini in a skillet with 2 tablespoons of butter. Sprinkle with freshly ground pepper. Cover with 3 tablespoons of Parmesan cheese; cover and cook slowly until the cheese is melted.

Rice Dodgers

2 cups warm cooked rice	flour
2 eggs, beaten	fat
½ teaspoon salt	

Add eggs and salt to warm, not hot rice. Mix well. Cool and form into cakes. Dredge with flour and cook on a well-greased hot griddle until golden brown.

Garbanzos (chick peas, the Mexican substitute for potatoes)

2 cups chick peas
1 clove mashed garlic
1 teaspoon salt

Soak peas overnight in salted water. Drain and rinse several times. Pour into 2 quarts of boiling water; add salt and garlic. Simmer covered for two hours.

Broiled Tomatoes

4 large ripe tomatoes
butter
basil

salt
pepper

Wash tomatoes, slice in half, top with a tiny nut of butter. Sprinkle with chopped basil leaves, salt, and pepper. Place on a grill over not too hot coals and broil until the tomato skin begins to become wrinkled. Serve at once.

Rice Pilau

1 tablespoon margarine
1 small finely chopped onion
1 cup uncooked long-grain rice

2 cups boiling chicken stock
1 teaspoon salt
1 tablespoon butter

Melt margarine in a low pot with cover. Sauté the onion until golden brown. Add the rice, salt, and boiling stock. Cover tightly and cook over medium heat for 30 minutes. Mix in the butter and serve. Mushrooms or cheese may be added. Serves 4.

Boiled Rice

1 cup washed raw rice
1 teaspoon salt
2¼ cups boiling water

Follow instructions on the package. They are usually very good. Or add the rice and salt to the boiling water. Bring to a rolling boil. Cover tightly and place over low heat. Cook for 25 minutes, or until all the water has been absorbed.

Saffron Rice (yellow rice)

Follow the directions for boiled rice, adding a good pinch of saffron after rice is started.

Wild Rice

½ pound wild rice
salt
¼ cup butter or margarine

Clean rice thoroughly through many waters. Let stand in water for 2 hours. Bring to a boil 1 quart of salted water. Add rice, cover, and cook slowly until done (about 30 minutes.) Drain and add ¼ cup of butter. Cover and steam for 5 minutes. Serves 6.

Hominy and Fried Hominy

2 cups hominy grits
5 cups boiling water
1 tablespoon salt

Soak the hominy overnight. Put water in a large kettle, and when water is fiercely boiling add the hominy and salt. Cook over a low flame for 1 hour, stirring often. Serve with gravy or a large pat of butter. This makes a wonderful substitute for potatoes.

To fry: pack the cooked grits into an open can and cover. Chill overnight. Cut into ½-inch slices and fry slowly in butter or fat. *Or:* beat one egg until lemony, add salt, pepper, and a dash of onion salt. Dip the hominy slices into the egg mixture and then in bread crumbs and fry slowly until golden brown.

9. Bread

Remove the staff of life from the "distaff-side" of the kitchen. Dazzle your hungry court with hot pones, dodgers, biscuits or hush puppies. Serve them up with plenty of butter and your reputation as King of the grill and skillet will reign supreme.

BREAD, FLAPJACKS AND SANDWICHES

Including a Group of Ingenious Over-the-Fire Recipes

Hoe Cake (a real slave recipe)
    2 cups corn meal
    water
    fat

Mix corn meal with cold water to form a soft dough. Then take a handful and toss it from one hand to the other over and over again into a long pone. Clap it down on hot greased "hoe" (griddle to you). Pat the cakes to about ½ inch thick. Brown on both sides and serve with plenty of butter.

Fried Co'n Pone
2 cups corn meal   hot water
½ teaspoon salt   ¼ piece salt pork

Sift corn meal and salt. Add hot water to make a thick, sticky dough. Try out the salt pork in a cast-iron skillet. Drop tablespoons of dough into the hot fat to make small pones. Brown on both sides, drain, and serve hot.

Spider Bread

1½ cups corn meal
2 tablespoons sugar
1 teaspoon salt
2 beaten eggs

1 teaspoon baking soda dissolved in 1 tablespoon cold water
1 pint sour milk
2 tablespoons butter

An hour before making bread, mix meal, sugar, salt, and sour milk in top of double boiler, cook over hot water 10 minutes and cool slightly. Stir soda dissolved in water into corn meal mixture. Stir in eggs. Melt butter in spider or bottom of Dutch oven. See that it is evenly spread. Put in the corn-meal mixture and cook over low heat about 40 minutes. Turn out on plate and add a little more butter to bottom of skillet or Dutch oven. Turn the bread back upside down to brown on second side for 10 minutes. Serve hot with butter.

Corn Dodgers

2 cups corn meal
1 teaspoon salt
1 egg

½ teaspoon sugar
2 cups boiling water
fat or shortening

Sift corn meal, sugar, and salt together. Add beaten egg and mix. Add boiling water. Beat thoroughly. Dip hands into cold water and form into small moist cakes. Heat 1 inch of fat in a large heavy skillet. Fry quickly. Lift with a spatula. Serve with butter. Maple syrup is very complementary.

Fried Mush

Pack leftover corn-meal mush or other cooked cereal into a beer can from which the top has been removed intact. Cover and leave in refrigerator overnight. Slice thin and sauté slowly on a greased skillet. Serve with maple or corn syrup or honey.

Hush Puppies

The story goes around Savannah that when the big out-door fish fries were held the neighboring dogs would smell the aroma of the food. To quell their howling and barking, the chef would make up a batch of pones which he would toss to the dogs, saying "Hush, puppies!" These delicious corn-meal nuggets became very popular throughout the South, and can now be purchased in prepared mix.

2 cups corn meal	2 cups milk
2 teaspoons baking powder	1 beaten egg
1 teaspoon salt	fat

Sift the dry ingredients and stir in egg and enough milk to make a thick, sticky dough†. Heat one inch of fat and fry nuggets about the size of a walnut in deep fat until they are a rich, golden brown. Drain on brown paper and serve hot.

Skillet Biscuits

2 cups biscuit mix
½ cup milk
shortening

Sprinkle some milk over biscuit mix and stir. Add more and stir; continue until the dough is soft but not soggy. Grease a 10-inch cast-iron skillet. Preheat. Spread the dough evenly in skillet. With a spatula, deeply crease dough every 2 inches in both directions like a checker board. Place over low heat and bake until done, when a testing straw comes out clean (about 12 to 15 minutes). Divide into squares. Serves 6.

† 1 cup of finely minced clams may be added.

Skillet-Bread Pizza

Proceed as above, but do not crease dough. Cover with thin strips of sliced ham facing east and thin strips of Swiss cheese going north. Spread ½ cup chili sauce evenly over the top. Cover. Cook over low heat until lightly brown on the bottom and cheese melts. Cut into wedges and serve hot. Serves 4.

Garlic Bread

    1 long loaf French bread
    ¼ cup butter
    2 cloves garlic, crushed in garlic press

Slice a loaf of bread on the bias to bottom crust, being careful not to cut through. Soften butter or margarine. Cream with the garlic pulp. Brush each slice with mixture. Wrap in 2 or 3 thicknesses of wax paper. Heat in a moderate oven about 8 minutes. For a delicious variation, sprinkle grated Parmesan cheese between the slices. Serves 6.

Garlic Rolls

    1 dozen hard rolls
    ¼ pound butter
    3 cloves garlic, crushed in garlic press

Slice rolls in half lengthwise. Brush with melted garlic butter. Place two halves together again and heat in paper bag 10 minutes. Serves 6.

Grilled Garlic Bread or Rolls

Rub the surface of bread with several cut cloves of garlic. Heat butter or margarine in a griddle. Cut loaves in half lengthwise and sauté, cut side down, until golden brown. Cut into 3-inch pieces and serve.

For Non-Garlic Eaters

Follow any of the above recipes for French bread or rolls. Eliminate the garlic. The bread will be deliciously hot and buttery and wonderful for outdoor or indoor dining. Some delicate herbs creamed into the butter before spreading add to the flavor.

Sandwiches are Easier Than Bread

Clear the boards for action by eliminating rolls, butter, and, if you are fancy, butter plates and such. Make these quick bread-and-spread combinations the day before the barbecue party. They'll keep perfectly well in a plastic bag in the refrigerator and save last-minute effort and table confusion. On a hot day they are super-tasty served cold.

Bread and butter: soften butter and spread generously on one side of thinly sliced homemade white, pumpernickel, salty rye, nut bread, brown bread or cheese bread.

Cucumber: slice cucumbers thin and store in the refrigerator in salted water. Put between bread-and-butter sandwiches just before serving. Add a dash of salt and pepper, a dab of mayonnaise. Try them with pumpernickel or brown bread—delicious!

Bermuda onion: slice very thin and serve in a side dish for those who crave onion sandwiches.

Lettuce or watercress: an hour before serving, spread one side of bread-and-butter sandwiches with mayonnaise. Add watercress or lettuce, a dash of salt and pepper. Keep chilled until mealtime.

Egg sandwiches may be made in exactly the same way. Use thin egg slices.

Steak sauce butter: Cream 1/4 pound of butter with a mashed clove of garlic, 1 teaspoon steak sauce, 1 teaspoon finely chopped parsley, salt, and fresh pepper to taste. Spread on bread.

Cream cheese mixed with olives or nuts can be made into sandwiches long in advance.

Chopped crisp bacon and pickles makes a nice spread for barbecue meals.

Flapjacks

If you enjoy flapjacks, wait until the first morning you have them à la barbecue. The natural affinity of open air and the aroma of the tasty cakes may cause you to eat twice the usual amount!

2½ cups sifted flour
2 tablespoons sugar
5 teaspoons baking powder
1 teaspoon salt

2 beaten eggs
2 cups milk
4 tablespoons melted butter or margarine

Sift dry ingredients. Add beaten eggs, milk, and butter or margarine. Beat briskly until just blended. Don't mind the lumps. Slowly heat a large griddle. When a drop of water dances on it, rub with a salt bag (2 tablespoons of salt tied in clean thin cloth). With a ladle pour about ¼ cup of batter for each cake. Batter should bubble when it hits the griddle. Don't space the flapjacks too closely, because the batter will spread a little. Wait until the top is full of holes and the edges are crisp. Turn and bake about half as long on the second side. Serve at once with butter and syrup. This makes about 15 cakes.

Fancy Twists for Flapjacks

To the above mixture add
A. 6 finely chopped pecans;
B. 1 teaspoon cinnamon, a sprinkle of freshly ground nutmeg, and half cup of raisins;
C. 1 banana, sliced thin;
D. half a cup of blueberries;
E. or roll a hot buttered cake around a hot sausage and eat with your fingers.

Buckwheat Cakes

Use 1½ cups buckwheat flour and 1 cup of regular white flour in the preceding recipe.

Sour-Milk Pancakes

Reduce the baking powder to 2 teaspoons; use 1 teaspoon baking soda and 2 cups sour milk instead of sweet milk.

10. *Fruit*

The finale should be light and gay. At the end of a festive meal serve your guests fruit, prepared with imagination. Fruit is Nature's tastiest gift to the epicure, and the best possible dessert to end a meal eaten in the open.

Tropical Compote with Wine Sauce

1 package frozen pineapple
   cubes
2 sliced bananas
1 large grapefruit in sections

1 cup seeded Malaga grapes
½ cup sugar
⅓ cup sherry
2 tablespoons Madeira wine

Prepare fruit just before the barbecue. Add sugar and wine. Place in refrigerator to chill while grill work goes on. Serves 6.

Peach Melba

  peaches
  ice cream
  crushed and sweetened raspberries

For each person use one large canned peach. Fill center with vanilla ice cream. Make a ribbon of raspberries over the top.

Hawaiian Luau Dessert

2 pineapples
½ cup sherry
1 quart strawberries

1 freshly grated coconut
2 tablespoons super-fine sugar

The morning before your barbecue quarter the pineapples. Do not remove the foliage. Remove the yellow meat and dice. Pour sherry over the pineapple meat. Grate coconut. Store pineapple and coconut in refrigerator until ready to use. Just before guests arrive hull strawberries. Arrange platter or bowl with the pineapple greenery arranged as a garland around the outside. Refill with diced, sherried pineapple. Set the strawberries like colorful ribbons between pineapples and a heap of coconut in the center. Pour over any sherry or pineapple juice left and sprinkle with sugar. Serves 8.

It Was Fit for the Gods (Ambrosia)

1 cup strawberries
2 oranges
2 ripe bananas
½ small coconut

pinch of salt
⅓ cup powdered sugar
liquor

Wash and hull strawberries, cut in halves. Peel oranges and remove pulp and tissue. Cut into ¾-inch chunks, saving the juice. Peel bananas and cut into ½-inch discs. Grate coconut. Mix the fruit and juice. Sprinkle with salt and powdered sugar. Flavor with brandy, rum, sherry or curaçao. Chill. Serves 6.

This can be varied according to the season by substituting tangerines, pineapple, blueberries, raspberries, melons, etc.

Fruit Bowl for Dessert

This makes a beautiful arrangement if you study the sizes of platter and fruits to be used and place the fruit with care in circular or ribbon pattern; as good to taste as it is appetizing to look at. Run this up well in advance and serve chilled after the big meal. Use canned, frozen, or fresh fruits.

Fill hollows of peaches, pears, apricots, etc., with crushed strawberries, crushed raspberries, or blueberries. Arrange on sides or in center mounds of whole strawberries, seedless grapes, wedges of grapefruit, tangerines, or oranges (your choice). Garnish with mint or watercress. You may place beside the platter a dish of freshly grated coconut, a dish of whipped cream flavored with rum or brandy, or a dish of sour cream mixed with cream cheese and chopped nuts.

> SERVICE NOTE: *To keep fresh fruits, such as apples, pears, etc., from turning brown, dip or brush them with a well-mixed solution of water and lemon juice. This will keep them in their original blond state for an hour or so. This works well with avocado, too.*

Melon Boat

a large watermelon
1 canteloupe
1 honeydew melon
½ pint of blueberries

½ pint of thawed frozen strawberries with juice
¼ cup powdered sugar
1 bunch of fresh mint

Slice the top from the watermelon, leaving the best two-thirds of the shell intact. Remove the pulp, leaving a thin pink lining. Scoop out the other melons, saving the juice. Remove seeds. Cut the melon pulp into balls with a scoop. Place the melon balls in the watermelon shell. Add ¼ cup of chopped mint and the strawberries with juice. Pour in enough melon juice to "float" shallowly. This can be done the day before. Cover with wax paper and store in the icebox to chill. Just before serving, sprinkle with blueberries and powdered sugar. Garnish with fresh mint sprigs. Serves a crowd.

Cantaloupe Coupé

4 small ripe cantaloupes	1 cup red raspberries
1 cup diced fresh peaches	1 cup frozen blueberries

Hull raspberries and store fruit in refrigerator to chill. Remember to remove blueberries three or four hours before they are needed. At the last minute slice melons in half. Peel and dice peaches. Fill melon wtih mixed fruits and juice. Top with a sprig of mint. Serves 8.

Vary this recipe according to fruit in season or your grocer's deep-freeze box. A teaspoon of peach brandy or a tablespoon of orange juice may be added to each melon half.

Honey Balls with Cottage Cheese

Chill melons and cottage cheese. Split melons and fill hollow with cottage cheese. Serve with 1/4 wedge of lime.

Grilled Bananas

4 firm bananas

Place bananas in their skins on grill. Cook for 8 minutes, turning three times. A delicious substitute for potatoes.

Banana Nut Roll

It's fun to serve a dressed-up dish that doubles for both salad and dessert. This one is especially good for barbecue because it can be prepared long beforehand. It will always win a round of cheers for being delicious and lovely to look at.

2 bananas	1/3 cup mayonnaise
1/2 cup chopped walnuts	1 teaspoon lemon juice
1 can grapefruit sections	lettuce

Mix the mayonnaise and lemon juice. Halve the bananas in the middle. Roll in mayonnaise, then in chopped nuts. Place on a crisp cup-shaped lettuce leaf and surround with grapefruit sections. Put a dab of mayonnaise on the side. Sprinkle with paprika. Serves 4.

Apple Snow

2 egg whites
2 cups applesauce

Apple snow is a good dessert, as it can be prepared easily before the guests. Whip the egg whites until stiff and add enough cold sweetened applesauce to make a stiff mixture. Serves 4.

Strawberry Whip on Sponge Cake

2 egg whites
2 tablespoons powdered sugar

1½ cups crushed strawberries
sponge cake

Beat egg whites until stiff, sweeten with sugar and fold in the crushed berries. Serve cold. If you have the ingredients chilled in the icebox, this is easy to make outdoors when you're ready for it. Place on sponge cake. Serves 6.

Bananas with Lime Juice on Sizzling Platter

4 bananas
2 tablespoons brown sugar

2 tablespoons melted butter
1 large lime

Split the bananas. Arrange them on a 12-inch oval sizzling platter. Sprinkle with brown sugar. Add the lime juice and butter. Baste frequently. When the bananas are golden brown and the juice has thickened, they are ready to serve. This takes about 15 minutes. Serves 4.

Flaming Bananas

An extra treat: when the bananas are ready to serve, sprinkle with ⅓ cup of brandy and set aflame.

Apple Pie (by Ben Irvin Butler)

9 apples
1 cup sugar
2 teaspoons flour
1 teaspoon cinnamon
½ teaspoon nutmeg
dash salt

3 tablespoons liquid tea
1 tablespoon lemon juice
pastry made from 2½ cups
   flour
2 tablespoons butter

Beforehand Preparation: Pare, core, and slice apples. Mix sugar, flour, spice, salt, tea, lemon juice. Work flour and butter into pie dough.

At the Grill: Roll about two-thirds of pastry ⅛-inch thick and fit into a deep 10-inch Pyrex pie plate. Dribble spice mixture over apple slices placed in pastry-lined dish. Dot with bits of butter. Roll remaining dough in rectangle and cut into ½-inch-wide strips. Arrange strips lattice-fashion over fruit. Dampen edge of pie, place strip of pastry around rim, and press it with tines of fork. Bake pie in hot (450 degrees F.) oven 10 minutes, then reduce heat to moderate (350 degrees F.) and bake another 35 minutes. Tea added to spices gives the pie a *fresh* flavor. Preparation of the pie proves your showmanship . . . its aroma while baking and its final taste stamp you as an expert. Serves 6 or 8.

TRAY BOY: *sliced apples, sugar, spice, and lemon-juice mixture, butter, pastry ingredients*

Menu

We recommend Ben's pie to top off any good barbecue meal. It is the perfect complement to a good steak.

INDEX

286